The Telescoping of Generations

The Telescoping of Generations is an original perspective on the transmission of narcissistic links between generations. This attention to unconscious transmission gives fresh understanding of the psychic consequences of experiences such as genocide and terrorism.

Reviving classic psychoanalytical concepts with fresh meaning, Haydée Faimberg demonstrates how narcissistic links that pass between generations can be unfolded in the intimacy of the session, through engagement with the patient's private language. The surprising clinical cases described in this book led the author to recognize the analyst's narcissistic resistances to hearing what the patient does say, and what the patient cannot say. She goes on to explore the value of hearing how the patient listens to both interpretations and silence: To study family secrets and to reinterpret the Oedipus myth.

The Telescoping of Generations is cogent both with regard to clinical practice and on a broader front. Psychoanalysts and psychotherapists treating adults and children, family therapists and those with an interest in cultural studies will all find it relevant to their work.

Haydée Faimberg, MD, is a Training and Supervising Analyst of the Paris Psychoanalytical Society (IPA). She is in private practice in Paris, created the Conference on Intracultural and Intercultural Psychoanalytical Dialogue (IPA), chairs the Clinical Forum of the European Federation, and has co-chaired the British–French clinical meetings since 1993.

THE NEW LIBRARY OF PSYCHOANALYSIS
General Editor Dana Birksted-Breen

The New Library of Psychoanalysis was launched in 1987 in association with the Institute of Psychoanalysis, London. It took over from the International Psychoanalytical Library, which published many of the early translations of the works of Freud and the writings of most of the leading British and continental psychoanalysts.

The purpose of the New Library of Psychoanalysis is to facilitate a greater and more widespread appreciation of psychoanalysis and to provide a forum for increasing mutual understanding between psychoanalysts and those working in other disciplines such as the social sciences, medicine, philosophy, history, linguistics, literature and the arts. It aims to represent different trends both in British psychoanalysis and in psychoanalysis generally. The New Library of Psychoanalysis is well placed to make available to the English-speaking world psychoanalytic writings from other European countries and to increase the interchange of ideas between British and American psychoanalysts.

The Institute, together with the British Psychoanalytical Society, runs a low-fee psychoanalytic clinic, organizes lectures and scientific events concerned with psychoanalysis and publishes the *International Journal of Psychoanalysis*. It also runs the only UK training course in psychoanalysis that leads to membership of the International Psychoanalytical Association – the body that preserves internationally agreed standards of training, of professional entry and of professional ethics and practice for psychoanalysis as initiated and developed by Sigmund Freud. Distinguished members of the Institute have included Michael Balint, Wilfred Bion, Ronald Fairbairn, Anna Freud, Ernest Jones, Melanie Klein, John Rickman and Donald Winnicott.

Previous General Editors include David Tuckett, Elizabeth Spillius and Susan Budd. Previous and current Members of the Advisory Board include Christopher Bollas, Ronald Britton, Donald Campbell, Stephen Grosz, John Keene, Eglé Laufer, Juliet Mitchell, Michael Parsons, Rosine Jozef Perelberg, David Taylor, Mary Target, Catalina Bronstein, Sara Flanders and Richard Rusbridger.

ALSO IN THIS SERIES

THE NEW LIBRARY OF PSYCHOANALYSIS

General Editor: Dana Birksted-Breen

The Telescoping of Generations

Listening to the Narcissistic Links
between Generations

Haydée Faimberg

Routledge
Taylor & Francis Group

LONDON AND NEW YORK

First published 2005
by Routledge
27 Church Road, Hove, East Sussex BN3 2FA

Simultaneously published in the USA and Canada
by Routledge
270 Madison Avenue, New York NY 10016

Routledge is an imprint of the Taylor & Francis Group

Typeset in Bembo by
Keystroke, Jacaranda Lodge, Wolverhampton
Printed and bound in Great Britain by
TJ International Ltd, Padstow, Cornwall
Paperback cover design by Sandra Heath
Paperback cover illustration: 'Adam and Eve' by Dürer
© by Museo del Prado

This publication has been produced with paper manufactured to strict
environmental standards and with pulp derived from sustainable forests.

British Library Cataloguing in Publication Data
A catalogue record for this book is available from the British Library

Library of Congress Cataloging-in-Publication Data
Faimberg, Haydée.
The telescoping of generations : listening to the narcissistic links between
generations / Haydée Faimberg.– 1st ed.
p. cm. – (The new library of psychoanalysis)
Includes bibliographical references and index.
ISBN 1-58391-752-7 (hardcover : alk. paper) –
ISBN 1-58391-753-5 (pbk. : alk. paper)
1. Narcissism. 2. Intergenerational relations. 3. Psychoanalysis.
I. Title. II. Series: New library of psychoanalysis (Unnumbered)
BF575.N35F35 2005
150.19′5–dc22   2004020812

ISBN 1-58391-752-7 (hbk)
ISBN 1-58391-753-5 (pbk)

For Antonio, for our children, for our grandchildren.

CONTENTS

Contents

ACKNOWLEDGEMENTS

I want to express my gratitude to my husband for his support and participation in the process of making this book, beyond being the co-author of one of the chapters.

I am in internal dialogue with Willy Baranger, José Bleger, David Liberman, Jorge Mom and Enrique Pichon-Rivière who generously transmitted a way of thinking psychoanalytically; with Guillermo Maci who gave me an approach for reading Freud; with André Green from whose knowledge and exceptional clinical skill I benefit; with Piera Aulagnier, Jean Laplanche and Serge Leclaire with whom I had the privilege of following seminars. Listening to Bion has been decisive.

My debt to Joyce McDougall is special; she always generously encouraged me to write and to publish and gave me her time for reading and offering suggestions for many of my papers.

I am indebted to my editor Dana Birksted-Breen for her intelligent dialogue, patience and support. Michael Fineberg was always there to find the English word that would best represent my thinking. To our son, Eduardo, all my gratitude for his help.

The discussion of my work with colleagues from analytic groups belonging to different traditions has been a source of inspiration, as has the annual French–British clinical meeting that Anne-Marie Sandler and I have co-chaired since 1993.

I thank Dunod for allowing me by contract to keep all the rights for the papers included in *La Transmission Psychique entre Générations*; and *International Journal of Psychoanalysis, Contemporary Psychoanalysis, La Revue Française de Psychanalyse*, the *Monographies de la Revue Française de Psychanalyse*, Presses Universitaires de France and *Revista de Psicoanálisis* for their permission to reproduce the following: Chapter 1, 'The telescoping of generations: A genealogy of alienated identifications (1981/1985)', was first published in Spanish in *Revista de Psicoanálisis*, 42: 1042–56 (1985), under the title 'El telescopaje de generaciones: Genealogía de ciertas identificaciones'; and in English in *Contemporary Psychoanalysis*, 24: 99–118 (1988), under the title 'The telescoping of generations: Genealogy of certain identifications'. Chapter 2, ' "Listening to listening": An approach to the study of narcissistic resistances (1981)', was first published in French in *Revue Française de Psychanalyse*, 45: 1351–67 (1981), under the title 'Une des difficultés de l'analyse: La reconnaissance de l'altérité: L'écoute des interprétations' (© PUF); and in English in the *International Journal of Psychoanalysis*, 77: 667–77 (1996) (© Institute of Psychoanalysis, London, UK). Chapter 3, 'Repetition and surprise: Construction and its validation (1989)' (written with Antoine Corel), was first published in *Revista de Psicoanálisis*, 46: 717–32 (1989) under the title 'Repetición y sorpresa: Una aproximación clínica a la necesidad de la construcción y de su validación'; and in English in the *International Journal of Psychoanalysis*, 71: 411–20 (1990) under the title 'Repetition and surprise: A clinical approach to the necessity of construction and its validation' (© Institute of Psychoanalysis, London, UK). Chapter 4, 'The countertransference position and the countertransference (1989)', has been published in the *International Journal of Psychoanalysis*, 73: 541–7 (1992) under the same title (© Institute of Psychoanalysis, London, UK). Chapter 5, 'The narcissistic dimension of the Oedipal configuration (1993)', was first published in Spanish in *Revista de Psicoanálisis*, 50: 901–17 under the title 'La dimensión narcisista del Edipo'. Chapter 6, 'The Oedipus myth revisited (1993)', was first published in French in René Kaës, Haydée Faimberg, Micheline Enriquez and Jean-José Baranès (1993), *La Transmission de la vie psychique*, Paris: Dunod. Chapter 7, ' "Listening to listening" and *après-coup* (1993)', articulates two articles: 'Pour une théorie (non narcissique) de l'écoute du narcissisme: Comment l'indicible devient-il dicible?', published in French in *La Psychanalyse: Questions pour Demain* (© PUF, 1990), Monographie 1, Presses Universitaires de France and 'Listening to listening' published in English in the *International Journal of Psychoanalysis*, 77: 667–77 (1996). Chapter 8, 'Misunderstanding and psychic truths (1995)', was published under the same title in the *International Journal of Psychoanalysis*, 78: 439–51 (1997) (© Institute of Psychoanalysis, London, UK). Chapter 9, 'Narcissistic discourse as a resistance to psychoanalytical listening: A classic submitted to the test of idolatry (2001)', was published in Spanish in *Revista de Psicoanálisis*, 61: 149–57 (2004) under the title 'Idolatría y discurso narcisista como resistencia a la escucha analítica'. Chapter 10, '*Après-coup*: Revisiting what has been read', has basically been written for this book. It is based partially on an article presented in 1998, which is to be published in the *International Journal of Psychoanalysis* in 2005 (© Institute of Psychoanalysis, London, UK). Chapter 11, ' "The Snark was a Boojum": Reading Lewis Carroll (1977)', was first published in English in the *International Review of Psychoanalysis*, 4: 243–9 (1977) under the title 'The Snark was a Boojum' (© Institute of Psychoanalysis, London, UK).

I want to thank the Museo del Prado for giving me permission to reproduce *Adam and Eve* by Dürer, whose copyright is acknowledged.

INTRODUCTION

G. K. Chesterton was fascinated by closed spaces – into which there can be no entrance and out of which there can be no egress – and by the way a crime could, in these conditions, be committed. In the tale entitled 'The invisible man', an enigma is presented where it appears that nobody has entered or left the house in which the murder occurred. 'Who is Nobody?' is the implicit question formulated to himself by Father Brown, after reflecting that, if a lady says that 'Nobody is listening to our telephone conversation' while a maid is in the room, she may not necessarily be lying. The answer might merely mean that there is 'Nobody' whom she would care about; of the 'same social condition', adds the Chestertonian priest maliciously and subversively. In the case of this crime there is nobody who could ever *be* considered responsible. The murderer, a postman, belongs to the invisible environment of everyday life. So we see that 'Nobody' is 'Somebody' who does not belong to the world of the person who is speaking – he does not count, he is invisible. However, he becomes visible when he is contemplated from a different point of view. It is not a question of seeing well or poorly; here we are more concerned about the conditions that allow something to become visible and somebody to become capable of seeing it.

Freud constructed a new theoretical object: the concept of the Unconscious and a new method for gaining access to this world. With this concept, an 'invisible man', an invisible object takes shape. Hysterics were considered as 'liars' until their truths became audible and the unconscious scene evident. After all, when Freud said that he had discovered something evident, namely infantile sexuality, he was pointing to this paradoxical phenomenon: We do not see what is so evidently there. Edgar Allan Poe in a masterful way showed us that the best way to hide a letter was to leave it where it could be seen.

This book deals with different kinds of 'invisible' object and 'inaudible' discourse. The theoretical object in psychoanalysis is not what we could call a natural object; it has to be constructed. And then, and maybe only then, it becomes something 'visible' – and audible – in the psychoanalytical session.

1

Transmission between generations is often such an 'invisible' object in psychoanalysis. We have a glimpse of it in almost every psychoanalytical writing, but perhaps in ways that do not allow us to grasp the essential presence of this issue. My purpose is to make it obvious and necessary, both theoretically and clinically, in the psychoanalytical experience of the session.

Another 'invisible' object, a complementary one, so to speak, is the narcissistic regulation of the object. I speak of narcissistic regulation in the sense of 'maintaining a certain regime', as it is developed in the book. To my knowledge, the narcissistic modality had not been attached to a particular kind of regulation, the functions of appropriation and intrusion.

In my approach, both concepts – the links between generations and the narcissistic object regulation – are intimately interrelated. However, in psychoanalysis it is not so much a question of seeing, as of listening. The analyst listens to the patient who in turn listens to the analyst's interpretations and/or silence. Then the analyst listens to the fate of his reinterpretations or silence. 'Listening to the [patient's] listening' has become a leitmotiv in my theoretical and clinical exploration: Listening to the telescoping of generations.

I have been working on the themes developed in this book since 1970. At that time I found that my patients, Jacques and Mario, led me to listen to something surprising – over and beyond what is continually surprising in the discovery of the unconscious world. I came to the conclusion that what my patients had to say or could not say were clinical answers to theoretical questions that I had yet to formulate.

It is as a result of this conclusion that I began writing this book, which presents a perspective (I think I should not call it a 'method') for searching for questions prompted by what the patient both tells and cannot tell us; by what we as analysts hear and cannot hear; and by what cannot be said but 'insists' as repetition and invites us to propose a (re)construction.

Even if this search began by commenting on another pursuit, on Lewis Carroll's 'The Hunting of the Snark', we may consider that my search for questions was launched in 1981 with two articles that have become the two leading chapters of the present work (Chapters 1 and 2). There I propose the hypothesis that the narcissistic modality and the unconscious identifications in which three generations are telescoped can be found in every analysis. In the subsequent chapters (written later, at the dates indicated) I return to these questions, but consider them in different clinical perspectives. Between the first two articles and the present time of writing these lines, a generation has elapsed! All this allows me to say that the bulk of this book was written in a span of 25 years.

As I explain in Chapter 9, what now may appear obvious was not at all obvious to me at that time. The original dates allow the reader to follow a step-by-step experience, familiar to all analysts, that goes from clinical experience to theory building and from theory to enlarging our capability for psychoanalytic listening.

I experienced this very complex movement in which each step gives retro-active meaning to the others as a non-linear, dialectical sequence. *This movement, this way of thinking the problems, is also what I wish to share with my readers.* Paradoxically, this non-chronological movement is better grasped by knowing the dates of the conceptual turning points. I have therefore chosen to limit the reworking of the original articles to stylistic revision and the suppression of repetitive material.

In most of the chapters, answers from different perspectives are attempted to the following key questions: Can we propose a theory for listening to narcissistic links between generations *without espousing the Ego's narcissistic beliefs* of being, as Freud puts it, the 'master in its own house'? Can we propose a, so to speak, 'non-narcissistic theory' (i.e. *a theory that studies narcissism but does not espouse the Ego's narcissistic beliefs*) of listening to narcissism?

This book describes a journey that I compare to my quest for the 'Snark'. For those readers who do not remember too clearly what kind of object a Snark is and how it may be hunted, I recommend that they read the final chapter, 'The Snark was a Boojum'. Among other 'instructive lessons', they will see the important role played by nonsense in revealing the existence of other types of logic – the logic of the unconscious, and its trademark, humour.

Haydée Faimberg

Paris, September 2003

1

THE TELESCOPING OF GENERATIONS: A GENEALOGY OF ALIENATED IDENTIFICATIONS (1981/1985)*

I was first led to reflect on the topic discussed in this essay by a patient with an apparently empty, dead psyche. During the sessions he was inaccessible, absent. He hardly acknowledged my presence. I failed to find any interpretative means to make myself exist in his psyche, which would thereby allow me to accurately interpret his absence; the patient simply was not there to listen to me! My only function consisted in holding – in my countertransference – the anxiety of not understanding and not existing as an analyst in the patient's psyche (but therefore being unable to modify his emptiness, his psychical death).

Mario was a man of 30 who had the appearance of an adolescent. Although he was a student of science, he had serious difficulties in thinking; he lived in almost complete isolation and had never had a love affair. Sometimes he appeared contemptuous and distant, at other times he seemed overwhelmed by anxiety (which he did not communicate) or else he looked bewildered. At the time I met him, Mario was being treated in an institution. He always remained silent and looked like an inanimate object rather than a person, except for a slightly contemptuous manner. He was considered as extremely helpless and solitary by all the patients in the institution, but he never spoke of this.

At that time Argentina, the country where he was treated in the early 1970s, was going through one of its serious economic crises. People bought dollars as a means of protection against the devaluation of the currency. Mario, however, made no attempt to defend his money. He remained in his timeless routine of

---

* A shorter version was presented at the Paris Psychoanalytical Society on 17 November 1981. This version was presented at the International Psychoanalytical Congress, Hamburg, in July 1985.

'doing nothing', a crystallization of time and of his life, which, in the present situation, assumed a critical quality. However, he showed no signs of concern; he just persisted in his contemptuous and self-sufficient attitude.

In the session to be discussed, Mario's anxiety became evident for the first time. He said he would not be able to continue with his analysis because his salary was not enough to keep him until the end of the month. It was evident that he wished to go on with his analysis, but also that he was not prepared to adopt any economic measure to preserve it. He mentioned that someone who was trying to persuade him to buy dollars had asked him if he knew how much a dollar was worth. Mario had answered that a dollar was worth two pesos. While he was telling me this, he made a barely perceptible gesture with his hand, as if to make sure that something in his pocket was still there, a loving gesture accompanied by a tender and secret smile. At the same time, with an absent, indifferent attitude, he said his friend told him that a dollar was worth 5,000 pesos. He did not seem concerned that he did not know the value of the dollar, neither was he shocked by his own mistake. He seemed to believe that it was the material reality that was 'wrong'.

The change in this session was that Mario expressed his desire to continue with his analysis; and his anxiety at the imminence of what he believed to be its inevitable loss. He was unconcerned with what might be called the material reality and was apparently unable to defend what he desired. Apart from the desire and the anxiety expressed in the transference, various other elements appeared, which can, with difficulty, be connected with one another:

1 Mario felt he was able to earn money with his work, but he was totally unable to protect it against inflation.
2 The purchase of dollars, which represented a method for preserving money against devaluation, seemed impossible in practice.
3 'Mario's dollars' were worth two pesos; those of material reality were worth 5,000.
4 Despite his being a science student, Mario was not at all surprised at his 'error of calculation'.
5 He lovingly caressed his pocket when talking about those 'two pesos' dollars, while he appeared to be indifferent as to the current value of the dollar.
6 Apparently he 'kept in his pocket' the secretly cherished and treasured 'two pesos' dollars.
7 To judge from their exchange value, those dollars belonged to *other times*, probably to the 1940s.

This was the first time I had so much interpretable material. However, all the elements refuted a certain kind of logic. If Mario's desire and his anxiety were to be related with the rest of the material, I could not make affirmative interpretations. All I could do is help us (the patient and myself) to formulate questions. I therefore said to him:

You must be keeping something very important in your pocket, something secret that demands your attention just when we are talking about the money you need to continue with me. You want to go on with your analysis and you are afraid of losing it. What demands your attention might be connected with the dollars that are worth two pesos. If such is the case, they must belong to some time in the past, perhaps to the forties. *I know nothing about this*, but *if* it were so, have you any idea *who* those dollars *are for?*' [While uttering my interpretation–construction, I realized that at that time Mario had *not yet been born*.]

Mario's answer motivated this essay. I realize that against the background of acknowledgement of Mario's desire and of his anxiety over the impending loss, I was making an interrogative construction. With it I communicated to my patient that I knew nothing about the object of the inquiry. It is through this construction–interrogation that we could begin to understand why such hetero-geneous elements, which did not follow an obvious logic (especially taking into account the date of Mario's birth), were linked together.

Mario's answer came immediately – a prompt, lively and personal answer. He talked with such a feeling of presence that there was no doubt that he was involved in what he was saying. We were engaged. He replied (as if it were natural and evident):

Yes, I know who those dollars are for. They are for my father's family. My father's family remained in Poland when my father left the country, in the thirties. My mother told me that my father's character completely changed after the emigration: he just stopped talking, in fact he never really learned Spanish. During the war he started sending money to his relatives in Poland every month, to his parents and his brothers and sisters. Dollars, it was dollars he sent. And a time came when nobody collected the money. I think the whole family had died. Well, my father never talked about them or what could have happened to them. I think he never really got to know what happened. It was my mother who told me all this.

The secret in the transference

Just as in other cases that I had in analysis later, Mario's history contained a secret. It was not a secret because of its content, since the patient himself talked about it in the session. However, I considered it a secret for at least three reasons. Some aspects of the parents' history, which he never spoke about, were mobilized by his account. The patient ignored the way in which he was involved in this secret history of his parents. The analyst was surprised during the session when a history she, the analyst, totally ignored was revealed to her.

6

How can two people talk about something when one of them (the patient) does not think it concerns him, and the other one (the analyst) is in ignorance of it? Complementarily, how can a patient be involved in a history that belongs to someone else?

The paradox is that Mario became present in his analysis when he spoke about what happened *before* he himself was conceived. *Why did he talk about this?* He did so, I believe, in order *to answer a question implicit in the transference*: Why, although he wished to, was he unable to protect his analysis financially? All this emanated from the interrogative construction. Nothing that Mario had said or done thus far revealed traces of what his father had silenced. Neither Mario nor the analyst possessed any clues that might allow them to wonder about the past, i.e. to acknowledge the secret. It was this quality that gave the patient's psyche its characteristic impression of emptiness and death.

There are key moments in an analysis when what apparently had no sense acquires meaning. I shall describe the conditions that are to be fulfilled if we are to achieve the almost clinical certainty that a secret history is part of the patient's psyche, and not just speculation constructed by the analyst, irrelevant to the transferential relationship.

I think it is of the utmost importance that in his countertransference the analyst should be able to bear the anxiety of not knowing and even of not knowing that he does not know. Only when, against this background of anxiety and ignorance, something as yet unrevealed in the patient's history is mobilized *to solve an enigma posed by the transference* do we reach the clinical quasi-certainty *that this history is part of the patient's psyche.*

I believe this clinical validation is supported by the following:

- The history is an answer to an explicit or implicit question of a transferential character.
- It provokes surprise and relief.
- The patient is effectively involved in the history: He addresses the analyst in such a way that the latter can understand the transferential quality.
- The analyst, on her side, experiences relief from her countertransference anxiety and the sudden realization of something that she did not know before.
- This 'not knowing' on the part of the analyst guarantees that it is the patient's history that becomes the organizer of new meanings.
- Therefore, the interpretation or construction is not based on something that was known beforehand.
- *Neither has the analyst been listening to the patient from the perspective of some previous knowledge.*
- The new meaning resulting from the secret fragments leads the analyst to a *retroactive* understanding of her own interpretation and the implicit question of the transference.
- She sees the psychical functioning of the patient differently.

7

- She understands differently who she, the analyst, *has been* for the patient thus far, from the point of view of transference.
- She learns something new that leads her to revise her implicit or explicit psychoanalytic theories.
- She is led to modify previous beliefs: These are privileged creative moments.

To sum up, Mario tells me, tells us, his secret history as an answer to the transference enigma as to why he cannot protect his treatment from a financial point of view. While telling his story, Mario shows that when he is apparently absent he is in fact elsewhere.

Where is Mario when he is absent?

It should be remembered that, until the session just quoted, I could not find a way of interpreting his psychical absence. Therefore this was a key question, but it could only be asked retroactively, after the session. The discovery that Mario was elsewhere made me realize that this was not only a psychical absence, but also the tyrannical intrusion of a history that concerned his father. In that sense, there was an 'overfullness', an object that was never absent.

Mario's analysis was threatened and aroused in him the desire to preserve it. On other occasions this desire was completely destroyed by his anxiety. In this way, Mario had crystallized in his psyche the situation of 'a father-who-does-not-acknowledge-the-death-of-his-family-in-Poland'. In his effort to protect his father's family from any passage of time connected with death, he maintained a form of inner death in his own psychical life.

How can we explain the transmission of a history that at least partially does not belong to the patient's life and that is clinically revealed (under the conditions I have described) as a constituent of the patient's psyche? How can this double, contradictory condition of a psyche that is *empty* and at the same time '*overfull*' be accounted for? In other words: A failure to acknowledge the object relationship and at the same time an excessive or never absent object.

The telescoping of generations: A particular form of identification

Let us examine the process through which the inaudible crystallization of the patient's psyche was produced. It is an identification process with features that may be defined as follows:

1 These identifications are split off, therefore they cannot be heard by the analyst.
2 They only begin to be detected at a key moment in the transference.
3 The identifications become audible to the analyst with the discovery of a secret history.

4   Since a certain type of relationship between generations is implied in the identifications, the object of identification is in itself a *historical* object. Therefore, and this is essential, the identification necessarily includes in its structure fundamental elements of the history of this object. The identifications have *a cause,*[1] *a 'condition of possibility' and are not just simple initial data that require no explanation.*

5   Understanding the *history of the identifications* makes them more significant, more audible.

6   *In this kind of identification process, a history is condensed which, at least partially, does not belong to the patient's generation.* In this sense I speak of 'alienated identifications'.

7   This condensation of *three* generations is what I call 'telescoping of generations'. It is discovered with the unconscious identifications revealed in the transference.

The identification process and its fate

'I love, I am; I hate, you are.' Since this identification process should be explained and not taken as a mere initial datum, a metapsychological analysis of its causes will be attempted. The title of this section is a variation of Freud's title, 'Instincts and their vicissitudes' (Freud 1915), an article which will be the central point in my discussion, complemented by the concept of narcissism defined from a Freudian theoretical and clinical point of view.

In 'On narcissism: An introduction', Freud (1914b: 91) shows how the child can remain a captive of the narcissistic ideals of his parents and how the object relationship can be the heir of such narcissism. Moreover, the concept of help-lessness linked to the premature psychical organization of the child (*Hilflosigkeit*) is essential if we are to understand how the parents' narcissism comes to be anchored in the child's psyche. Acknowledging the child as a separate individual involves the parents in an active elaboration of their narcissism, in order to permit the child to work through a genuine oedipal position.

Elsewhere (Chapter 2), I have defined narcissism as:

> [T]he ego's love for itself and for objects, based upon its illusion of being the centre and the master of its world. The ego[2] loves itself as an object, and this love and this illusion are at the basis of the actual structuring process of the ego.

Like Michel Neyraut (in the discussion that followed my presentation in 1981) I would say that, on account of its origin, narcissism needs to be approved by the other: At the beginning by the mother and the father. In its own illusory assertion of itself, there is a contradiction because while it needs the other to confirm it, it declares: 'Look, I am self-sufficient.'

9

This accounts for the fact that, clinically, the relation is at once an object relation and a narcissistic relation. The narcissistic object relation does not tolerate anything from the object that does not evoke pleasure. On this is based, essentially, its narcissistic character. In order to appreciate this statement, let us continue with Freud in 'Instincts and their vicissitudes'.

Freud examines the different moments that enable the subject to differentiate himself from the object. According to the logic of narcissism, regulated by the principle of pleasure–unpleasure, the following equation is proposed. The ego is the equivalent of pleasure and the non-ego is the equivalent of unpleasure. This means that when the subject feels unpleasure he will tend to attribute it to a 'non-ego'; when the object provokes unpleasure the subject will tend to hate it. This narcissistic regulation explains, therefore, the difficulty in establishing the distinction between the objective and the subjective. In this way the non-ego becomes the logical antecedent of the object. When a narcissistic object relation is established, the principle of pleasure–unpleasure still rules, even if there is a distance between the object and the ego. This distance implies the acceptance of the object loss.

The parents of the patient can be seen, *not* from the point of view of material reality or of what they might have actually been like in the past, but as they are activated in the transference, that is, as something imprinted in the patient's unconscious psychic reality. This is eloquently shown in the way the analyst's interpretations are listened to. The patient often unconsciously identifies with those 'internal parents' who are the organizers of his psyche. This means that it is *the patient himself who functions according to a narcissistic regulation*. For this reason it is an *alienated* or split identification of the ego, insofar as its cause is partially found in the history of the 'other'.

The split or alienated part of the ego is *identified with the narcissistic logic of the parents* according to which: 'All that deserves to be loved is me, although it comes from you, the child. What I acknowledge as coming from you, the child, I hate; you, however, will be loaded with all that I do not accept in me: You, the child, will be my not-me.' When I say 'the child', I am referring to the libidinal and aggressive experience of the child and the acknowledgement of a psychical space of his own.

I call the 'appropriation' function the first 'moment' of narcissistic love and the 'intrusion' function the second 'moment' of narcissistic hatred. *The appropriation and intrusion functions are characteristic of the narcissistic object regulation.*

In the appropriation function the internal parents, when identifying themselves with what pertains to their child, appropriate for themselves his positive identity. In the intrusion function, when actively expelling into the child all that they reject, the internal parents define him by a *negative* identity. Thus the child is hated not only because he is different, but also, above all, and paradoxically, because his history will be congruent with the parents' history and with all that is not accepted by them in their narcissistic regulation. There is no psychical space here for the child to develop his own identity, free from the alienating power of the parents' narcissism.

This alienating function, as we have already noted, is the cause of a splitting in the child's ego (Freud 1927a, 1938a, 1938b) that produces an experience of estrangement. By estrangement, I mean both the feeling of estrangement and also the estranged organization that belongs to the other. In fact, that is the definition of alienation.[3]

Summing up, alienated identifications (alienated because they partially depend on conflicts of a generation that is not the patient's) respond to the mechanisms of appropriation and intrusion. This means that the patient's internal parents function in the framework of the narcissistic regime described earlier, in which they cannot love the child without appropriating his identity for themselves and they cannot acknowledge his independence without hating him and subjecting him to their own history of hatred.

With this reasoning we would be led to include at least two generations in the study of these identifications, but in the example we are considering, three generations are concerned. The parents themselves are not the only protagonists of the relationship, they are inscribed in an *unconscious* family structure. Therefore, in this type of identification *three generations* are always involved.

I love, I am: This means that I am the good object. I hate, you are: This means that you are the bad object. This may be the formula that will make it possible to define the dramatic situation in which the patient is alienated by his unconscious identification with the parents' way of functioning (linked to the parents' history, together with its anxiety and death).

I will not discuss the processes of projection and introjection here as such,[4] but only the conditions for a situation to take place in which: (a) The other appropriates the patient's psychic investments; (b) the patient becomes a captive of the other's intrusion.

Disidentification and time

The emergence in the transference of this type of identification is the starting point of a key psychoanalytic concept: Historicization. With the identification process the psyche is fixed in an 'eternity' characteristic of the unconscious in its quality of timelessness. It would be more accurate to speak of different forms of temporality. When the secret history is revealed, its effects on the ego can be modified. This means modifying the alienating splitting. With this process of disidentification (with respect to an alienated identification), history can be re-established with the quality of 'past'. Thus, disidentification (and, therefore, disalienation) is the condition for the liberation of desire and the constitution of the future.

11

In reference to time and desire, Freud wrote:

> By picturing our wishes as fulfilled, dreams are after all leading us into the future. But this future, which the dreamer pictures as the present, has been moulded by his indestructible wish into a perfect likeness of the past.
>
> (Freud 1900: 621)

Telescoping, as described in this essay, reveals a circular, repetitive time. The difference of generations, on the contrary, is connected with the inescapable passage of time and the distribution of generations. Something irreversible has occurred (as described by Michel Neyraut (1978)). This approach enables us to solve a theoretical impasse that has serious clinical consequences and could lead to remaining stuck in the following alternative: Either (a) considering identifications as a simple *illusion* of the ego and therefore omitting to listen to and to interpret this type of unconscious identification or (b) emphasizing the identification *with the analyst*.

My option is to interpret the unconscious identifications revealed in the transference inasmuch as they contribute to the formation of the psyche and inasmuch as they submit the patient to a history that (partially) does not belong to him and, indeed, alienates him. From this perspective, I consider legitimate the analytic work that liberates the analysand from this submission; it is a task accomplished from a virtual point of listening and interpreting the transference that allows disidentification.

My perspective is in no way concerned with adaptation to an identification model. On the contrary, it is the system of appropriation–intrusion proper to the narcissistic organization that forces the patient to an alienating adaptation. This perspective contributes *towards resolving the dilemma between interpreting in the present and interpreting in the past*. The so called 'past' *becomes past* because of the disidentification process: The sense of being outside the passage of time is overcome.

Now let us return to the twofold problem. How can the transmission of a history that does not correspond to the patient's generation be explained? How can the paradox of the patient's psyche – at the same time empty and overfull – be understood? The emptiness and the death of any desire in Mario found a cause in the appropriation process. The intrusion process was the basis for the ever-present object. Let me review Mario's session with this perspective in mind.

On the one hand, the intrusion process is responsible for the excessive presence, the object that is never absent. This object is made up of what had been actively expelled by Mario's father and which the son had to contain. The formulation corresponding to this intrusion might be the following: 'The death of my family is a reality I hate; I expel all of this into my living son whom I hate and reject.' This formulation corresponds to the unconscious fantasy that constitutes the 'not-me' of the father, which has become the condition of possibility (the cause) of Mario's alienating identification, i.e. Mario becomes the (father's) not-me. Defining himself in this way, he now acquires a *negative identity*. Yielding to this alien power, Mario's ego is split. This explains his perplexity and contempt. The contempt probably corresponds to the coexistence of two processes: The rejection of all reality that may threaten his identification *and*, parallel to this, the rejection of the history that has caused his identification. Silently and unconsciously, Mario identifies himself with this 'silent-father/ son-faced-with-a-family-that-never-collected-the-dollars-only-sign-of-their-death'.

On the other hand, complementarily, the appropriation process is cause of Mario's psychical emptiness and the death of any wish of his own that might endanger his father's family. Time must have an end point. He cannot desire the continuation of his analysis or buy dollars, because the transaction would mean buying-dollars-which-are-worth-five-thousand-pesos and not two pesos and admitting that 'those' dollars have not been collected: A death sentence.

I am not simply stating that the patient has unconsciously identified himself with his father. I think that an identification involving a telescoping of generations is carried out with the object and part of the attributes of the secret history and not only with the object in question. (May it be assumed that all identifications are made with the process and not only with the object?)

There is still another issue: The enigmatic way in which the history is transmitted. When Mario says, in reference to his father's history, 'It was my mother who told me', I do not believe he is talking about the transmission that brought about the unconscious identification. The maternal message does not have a stifling effect, but one of liberation; it was in fact the text that gave us the first hint towards understanding the origin of this identificatory capture. Contrariwise, the maternal message is insufficient to explain why most of the psyche should have organized itself around the identification process.

In the session to be examined next, the mother does not even appear as a messenger of her own history. The history is not transmitted in the form of an explicit message, but in connection with the parents' way of speaking and not speaking. This session took place a year later. Mario began by saying:

> I asked my mother about Auntie Rita. She was quite surprised at my knowing of her existence and asked me how I knew about her. I remembered her. I don't know if I had always remembered her, but in the last few years I realized I knew about her. My mother told me that Rita was confined to a psychiatric hospital. I asked her how long ago had she been sent there and she told me it had happened when she (my mother) was expecting my brother. I was five at the time. My mother never went to see my aunt and never talked about her. But my other aunt often went to see her. All this happened three months

ago, but for some reason I've been unable to tell you until now. During these three months I found out where she was and I asked my brother, who is a doctor, to see if she was well taken care of. I have been visiting her, telling her all that has happened in the twenty-five years she has been isolated from the world. I've taught her to wash [he said, pointing to his own shoes that, for the first time looked clean] and I've set myself as an example.

Mario added that in these three months he had asked his mother a lot of questions. She told him that 'when his brother was born Mario stopped playing and talking and he was never himself again'. Mario says he feels guilty at having hidden all this from me, but he just could not do otherwise.

My interpretations at different moments of the session might be summarized as follows:

You had to do everything secretly, because only in that way were you able to transmit the secret aspect of the question. You didn't know how to talk about a secret; all you could do was to subject me to the secret and 'exclude' me. In this way I would become the isolated person, who knows nothing, feels nothing, does not exist. That is how you felt, just like your aunt. But now you can say to yourself, say to your aunt, and say to me that time has passed, that you have a brother who is now a doctor.

I think the elaboration of paternal identifications permitted, one year later, the revealing of identifications connected with the mother's history. It may be assumed that the memory of the aunt's existence, together with all that Mario did in order to reintegrate her (even taking her out of hospital and bringing her to his own home) represented his acceptance of his mother's pregnancy and his brother's birth. The fact that he was able to express guilt feelings leads us to assume that I existed as an *excluded* person for him and that I had not been painlessly *suppressed from his existence*.

The mother had repudiated the existence of the aunt and this had happened when Mario should have gone through the experience of jealousy and exclusion evoked by his mother's pregnancy. But Auntie Rita did not exist neither did Mario, in feeling the exclusion, even feel jealous at his brother's birth. It was the very sibling identity that was denied in its existence. The exclusion was brought about in the being and not in the having. Mario was *thus identified with the non-existence of a sibling. By not talking, not playing, not being himself any more, he did not exist as a brother, and repudiated the birth of his own brother. The identification was produced in collusion with the mother's history.*

Thus the mother was not a messenger of her own history, which became a basis for Mario's unconscious identification. The history was not transmitted as an explicit message but, I believe, was closely connected with the parents' way of talking and not talking. The mother could only talk when Mario started disidentifying himself from the alienated aunt and was able to ask the necessary questions.

So far Mario had never talked about his parents with me, neither had he mentioned any conflict. All Mario's identity had been held captive through the internal parents' narcissistic organization. He had become what each of them had not accepted in their respective histories. Consequently, there was no distance between himself and his objects. Furthermore, there had been no acknowledgement of object loss. The threat of losing the treatment unleashed the process related to the object loss. From that moment, Mario began complaining about his helplessness and admitting conflict.

The identifications constitute a 'link between generations', which are alienating and opposed to any psychic representation; therefore they are not articulated and not heard by the analyst. The passage from identification to representation (as André Green noted in the discussion of the aforementioned lecture) became possible due to the interpretative construction. Let us re-examine this interpretation on the basis of what has been developed.

In the interpretation acknowledgement of personal desire is indicated. This is carried out with the comment, '[. . .] just when we are talking about the money you need to continue with me'. The 'we' means that I acknowledge Mario's desire to go on with his analysis and that I formulate the interpretation acknowledging my own desire to go on analysing Mario. Incidentally, it should be emphasized that the acknowledgement of my desire as an analyst may be inferred retroactively, precisely from the way the interpretation was formulated. The phrase 'your analysis with me' re-establishes the necessary dissymmetry in the psychoanalytic relationship.

The comment, 'You must be keeping something very important in your pocket, something secret that demands your attention just when we are talking about the money' means that I have discovered that Mario has 'made an investment somewhere else' (an investment in the financial sense as well as in the sense of libidinal and aggressive economy). I realize that in this formulation *I anticipate (as a clinical answer) a theoretical question that at the time I had not yet formulated.* That is, there is a certain type of splitting that alienates desire and prevents the subject from possessing his own desires. Although I mention his desire in the transference (that of continuing with his analysis), I also tell him, and this is important, that I do not know what 'the investment made somewhere else' means.

I now realize that I defined an aspect of our relationship of which Mario was unaware. This consists in accepting that 'I am excluded from his secret' and admitting that 'I don't know'. In the interpretation exclusion is implicitly differentiated from suppression. Therefore, I have anticipated the capacity that Mario will gradually develop for being jealous instead of suppressing his brother's existence, suppressing in himself the capacity for feeling, as Auntie Rita's existence had been suppressed. But more important than my accepting being

15

excluded is the fact that I acknowledged that Mario possessed a secret. Seen in the light of narcissistic regulation, this meant that, unlike his parents, I accepted that he should possess a personal, secret space. (Here this secret implied the overcoming of the parents' secret.) Of course, I was unaware of all this at the time.

Since his space is personal, I told him that only he could answer my question, because *I did not know*. This interpretation defined us as two different people and this put into question his megalomania (or mine in the transference); I needed his associations so that we could know. However, and this is the weakest point in my construction, I proposed to him a representation that came from me (the relationship between the dollar at two pesos and the 1940s). This pre-conscious representation came from my own personal history, although I purged the significance that it had for me. I kept the inquiry open without communicating the perplexity I experienced when I realized – while I was posing my construction – that at that time Mario had not yet been born. I must admit that Mario's answer legitimized this rather dubious part of my interpretation. When I formulated it, I had been afraid of 'going too far' with my hypothesis on the value of the dollar. Last, in the interpretation I stressed that I knew nothing about the investment he had made elsewhere, but if he knew something about it, perhaps he also knew for whom that investment (as well as those dollars) were meant.

We are dealing with an unconscious level, where the object of desire remains secret. In the transference, there are two contradictory desires: The desire to continue with the analysis and the desire to remain bound to a secret history. Anxiety arises from these two conflicting desires. The desire/identification dialectic begins to be expressed and at the same time the alienating identifications become articulated. I think it is unnecessary to add that the interpretation does not describe behaviour, that Mario's gesture was included in an unconscious chain of meanings as the missing link. It is precisely this unconscious meaning that enables us to talk of interpretation.

At this point, I should like to propose a crucial theoretical question: *Can we talk of narcissism without a narcissistic theorization? In other words, is it possible to adopt a position at a different level from the narcissistic theories of the patient?* I would like to be able to do so, since I believe that the oedipal situation cannot be neglected. The alienating unconscious identifications (caused by the intrusion and appropriation functions characteristic of narcissistic regulation) make up the 'narcissistic dimension of the Oedipus'[5] (temps narcissique, Maci 1979).

Mario believed he could live without libidinal and aggressive exchanges with the other. He stopped time and this megalomania formed part of his narcissistic conception of himself. However, there is still the intrinsically contradictory character of narcissism, which, while claiming to be self-sufficient, needs the confirmation from the other. The traumatic reality of the rapid inflation in Argentina forced Mario to admit that his precious dollars did not allow him to pay for his analysis (it is easy to understand the hatred mobilized against me by this narcissistic wound) and last, he had to admit that those dollars had not been of any use in keeping his father's family alive and that even his own psychical life was in mortal danger. The 'living-dead' (Baranger 1961) threatened his wish to continue with his analysis, a conflict expressed in the transference by anxiety.

The narcissistic dimension of the Oedipus first becomes available to analysis when the process of disidentification begins. At first Mario talked about his father using his mother's words. This means that in Mario's psyche the mother is saying: 'Already before your birth I lost the man that I had chosen for a husband.' 'With the migration he stopped talking and was never himself again.' Then Mario talked about himself in reference to his brother's birth and he again uses his mother's words: 'When your brother was born, you stopped playing and talking, and you were never yourself again.' It should be recalled that when his mother was pregnant (with his brother) she stopped talking about her own sister, Aunt Rita. We assume that the mother was never the same again for Mario. It should also be remembered that Mario's disidentification with the alienated aunt enabled him to ask his mother the right questions and receive the right answers.

The mother (in Mario's psyche) as a messenger of the Oedipal organization talked about Mario's father and about Mario in the *same* terms and this was used by Mario in an omnipotent way to *resist* the wound provoked by the oedipal conflict: The father appears *like a brother* with whom he is in rivalry, they are two silent, bewildered children before the mother who describes them as 'changed'. The alienating identifications provided the structure that allowed this process to take place. From that time onward, Mario was able to analyse his relationship with his father, who stopped being only the *grandfather's son* and came alive as *a father* in Mario's inner world.

Let us revisit what has been said up to now. The discovery of a special kind of identification (alienated identification) opens the path to historicization. The patient achieves the possibility of disidentifying himself and of finding his place with regard to the difference of generations. This type of identification implies a 'telescoping of three generations'. This reflection is centred on the relationship existing between parental narcissism and the process of unconscious identification.

If the parents' narcissistic love means taking away from the child what gives him pleasure, as a consequence, when the child differentiates himself, they hate him. But there is an additional complication that was manifested in Mario's case. What the parents hate in the child is also what they hate in themselves. Bion (1962a, 1962b, 1965), Klein (1945, 1946, 1952) and Winnicott (1947), among others, have addressed this idea.

The paradoxical consequence is that this difference, this separation, tends to disappear. In Mario's case, his identity was determined by what had been excluded from the history of the parents; his identity remained, therefore, in solid connection with this history and since it was organized under the *aegis* of negation, it can be labelled a negative identity. In a previous paper (Faimberg 1976), I showed how the threatening absent object, not symbolized yet as a lost object, is *a present non-object*. I also stated that this *non-object constituted the determined negation of the object*. In the present study, I develop a complementary aspect, namely that the *ego finds in the non-ego the negation determining its identity, which is, in consequence, a negative identity*. The patient's basic affirmation (*Bejahung*) is built on the model of expulsion, the fundamental negation of the internal parents.[6]

To free oneself from the narcissistic control of the internal parents, a possible solution consists in defining oneself as the hated one, in order to achieve separateness. Another solution (as in Mario's case) consists in assimilating oneself to all that is hated in the parents' history, that is, by defining oneself as undifferentiated. The first solution, even though it is achieved through hatred, maintains the distance between the ego and the object; in the second, this distance that characterizes object loss is not established. We are not examining here the relations between these identifications, on the one hand, and the ego and the superego as instances, on the other. To examine them would have required widening the discussion to include the relation between the appropriation–intrusion system and repression, on the one hand, and the relation between the narcissistic level and the oedipal level, on the other. Only a partial analysis was made when we referred to the narcissistic dimension of the Oedipal organization.

The question still remains as to whether the telescoping of generations can be explained in every case by the appropriation and intrusion functions, which we have defined as characteristic of narcissistic regulation. In addition, considering the cases of other patients whose conflicts are compatible with the analysis of a classical situation, as is the case of Jacques with the analysis of a dream (see Chapter 3), we might also question whether the telescoping of generations is not a universal phenomenon that might be interpreted at some stage or other of any analysis. If such were the case, many phases of anxiety might be better understood when facing situations of change that demand a restructuring of identity, as well as many enigmatic situations with a negative therapeutic reaction.

Between the intrusion and the appropriation, between emptiness and an ever-present object, psychoanalytic interpretation seeks to establish the presence, embodied in the words required to name the absence.[7]

'LISTENING TO LISTENING': AN APPROACH TO THE STUDY OF NARCISSISTIC RESISTANCES (1981)*

Psychoanalysis provokes in mankind a narcissistic wound, calling into question the illusion of the ego of being 'master in its own house' (Freud 1917b: 143). We naturally encounter some conscious productions corresponding to this illusion of the ego. And the ego resists accepting any knowledge likely to cast doubt on this illusion: Freud studies this resistance as an *epistemological* obstacle. It is therefore reasonable to suppose that this obstacle may be found inside the psychoanalytical process itself.

I shall examine certain forms of resistance that are manifested in the transference. I define these as *the resistances that the ego puts up during the analysis faced with the disillusion of not being the centre and the master of its world.* Transference proved to be an unavoidable but fecund obstacle for Freud, on *condition* that it was not ignored (he learned this from Dora in a radical way). Similarly when considering the obstacle furnished by the ego I will do this following Freud's method, i.e. working on the obstacle itself.

I shall define this obstacle as narcissistic, giving the term narcissistic a precise connotation: *The ego's love for itself and for its objects, based on the illusion of being the centre and the master of its world.* The ego loves itself as an object and this love and this illusion form the basis of the *actual structuring process of the ego.*

The ego in fact refuses to recognize the following:

1 The impossibility for the subject to beget himself, i.e. that the world existed before him, the difference between generations.

---

* Translation, with minor modifications, of the text published in French in 1981.

2 The difference between the sexes (recognising that *each* sex reflects the other as *incomplete*[1]).

3 Otherness.

In other words, the ego refuses to accept *the wound inflicted by the Oedipus conflict*. This resistance seems even more important in that it can present itself as totally accepting the analytic situation, thereby giving the illusion that what is usually called 'therapeutic alliance' spontaneously exists. The concepts of 'therapeutic alliance', 'autonomous ego' and 'conflict-free area' tend to be in solidarity with what the ego wishes to believe. More than concepts linked to narcissism, they reinforce the narcissistic beliefs themselves.

The problem consists in knowing whether we can take into account the narcissistic functioning of the patient and its forms of resistance as revealed in the psychoanalytic situation without making an implicit theorization that is in accordance with the ego's beliefs. Such a theorization would have to take into account the recognition of the difference between generations, of the difference between the sexes and of otherness, in order to be in a position that differs from that of narcissistic beliefs: It must be able to refer to narcissism, without being itself a narcissistic discourse. I am thus approaching the following problem: How can one *listen* to the manifestations of *narcissistic resistance during a session*? Otherwise formulated, how can one listen to the different ways in which the patient's narcissistic love is preserved, a preservation that is related to the ego's belief that it is the centre and 'the master in its own house'? I shall briefly summarize the theoretical horizon on which my reflections are based.

Freud underlines the narcissistic nature of the love for the object in the relationship between the *parents* and the child:

> Parental love, which is so moving and at bottom so childish, is nothing but the parents' narcissism born again, which, transformed into object-love, unmistakably reveals its former nature.
>
> (Freud 1914b: 91)

Furthermore, because of its state of helplessness (*Hilflosigkeit*), the child is drawn to graft itself onto the parents' narcissism. In 'Instincts and their vicissitudes', Freud (1915a: 136) refers to the 'purified pleasure–ego' and states that the ego is identified with that which produces pleasure, even if the pleasure comes from the outside world. Anything which produces unpleasure is attributed to the outside world, even if unpleasure comes from within.

> If later on an object turns out to be a source of pleasure, it is loved, but it is also incorporated into the ego; so that for the purified pleasure–ego once again objects coincide with what is extraneous and hated.
>
> (Freud 1915a: 136)

In the same article, Freud tells us that hate is the (logical) antecedent of the object.

Hate, as a relation to objects, is older than love. It derives from the narcissistic ego's primordial repudiation of the external world.

(Freud 1915: 139)

For the sake of clarity, I shall state again the unconscious fantasy with which patients relate to their 'internal parents'. From a clinical point of view, the formula that best reflects the narcissistic regulation of these parents would be the following:

1   The only one worthy of love is me – say the internal parents – even if what is loveable comes from the child.
2   I tend to hate that which I recognize as coming from the child; furthermore, I shall expel into the child all that I do not accept in myself: The child is my not-me.

As we know, we speak of the 'internal parents' as they are inscribed in the patient's psyche – and as they are recreated in the transference – and not the parents of material reality. I have defined elsewhere (Chapter 1) the functions of appropriation and intrusion. I call the appropriation function the first 'moment' of narcissistic love and the intrusion function the second 'moment' of narcissistic hatred. The appropriation and intrusion functions are characteristic of narcissistic object regulation. In consequence, and this is important, in the narcissistic object relation *only hate defines otherness*.[2]

The key question of this study may be expressed in a nutshell: How can we, as analysts, hear the narcissistic dimension of the Oedipal configuration during the sessions? To develop this question I shall proceed directly to the central thesis.

The forms of narcissistic resistance that present the greatest obstacle to the psychoanalytical process are those arising from the determination of the patient's identity, an identity that results from the narcissistic struggle with the internal parents as they are reproduced in the transference.

I would also add, as a complementary postulate, that ideally the parents' Oedipal functioning should support the *recognition of the child in his otherness* and the listening and interpretations of the analyst are also ideally situated in an Oedipal position. I propose to study *the effect of the predominance of the narcissistic links of the mother and also of the father as revealed in the transference, in relation to the Freudian notion of 'me/not-me'*.

Patients who partly lack a narcissistic constitution, due to the fact that the parents did not provide an Oedipal support, paradoxically hear the analyst's interpretations through a narcissistic reinterpretation. They repeat, in the transference, the narcissistic struggle through which they establish their identity.

21

This struggle may be defined as a struggle in which each ego keeps its love for itself based on the belief that it is the centre of its world and thus omnipotent – a belief that persists even in the narcissistic object relationship. The child, in this way, forms a triangle with the parents: Each point of the triangle constitutes a not-me for the other two; and the values of each 'me' attributed to the other as 'not-me' do not necessarily coincide. (We shall return to this point.)

Given the over-determination of what is meaningful in a session, I shall choose one perspective among the others, which are all just as fundamental. More precisely, I shall centre my remarks on the narcissistic logic (*le temps narcissique*) whereby the ego resists in order to deflect the wound inflicted by the oedipal situation. The oedipal conflict is therefore an unavoidable implicit point of reference and my study is based on the 'narcissistic dimension of the Oedipal conflicts'.

Manifestations of resistance on the part of patient and analyst

A common example of narcissistic resistance centred on the illusion of the perception of consciousness is revealed in the case of the patient who responds to an interpretation (which is neither ineffective nor frankly erroneous) with the statement: 'I don't see it that way', which frequently really means: 'I don't see it that way, because your interpretation produces an unpleasant feeling in me; as a consequence, I wish to expel it, I reject this interpretation, my associations and even your existence: This psychic reality does not belong to me – it is "*not-me*", I don't feel it.' The analyst, for his part, occupies the position of a decentred listener; but this decentred position does not necessarily protect him from the effects of such narcissistic beliefs; his own and those of the patient.

The theory, essential in this case, can be narcissistically reappropriated by the analyst in two different ways. The first consists in selecting the elements that allow us to nurture the illusion according to which our theory is complete, trustworthy and permits us to be totally in command. We would then have a *tautological-narcissistic listener*. I do not wish to suggest, however, that it is possible to believe in 'natural' analytical material, empirical and independent of all theoretical construction. I am referring to the narcissistic obstacle that the analyst may put up to listening to something that threatens his ego's illusion of omniscience *built on his theory*.

There is a second, more subtle difficulty: Although the analyst's theory may include the incompleteness of the ego, the analyst listens and/or interprets so as not to disillusion the patient, but to such an extent that the patient maintains the illusion that the analyst knows and knows so much that the patient's associations and psychic working through are superfluous. From this point of view, simply by speaking the patient provides a refutation to the illusion that the analyst knows everything. Conversely, certain silences on the part of the patient may be understood in terms of the disillusion at having to speak. The patient therefore persists in the illusion that he has a self-sufficient ego, an ego that is, in fact, represented by the analyst himself. The omniscient analyst would then represent the patient's ideal ego and at the same time, the analyst would see his own illusion recreated and covered on this occasion by his theoretical position. In this way, the basis of a reciprocal narcissistic fascination would be constituted.

At certain moments, such reciprocal fascination is sustained by an interpretation that validates what the patient's narcissistic discourse wants to impose. At other moments, silence itself can produce the same effect. Winnicott rightly suggested that interpretation restricts the illusion of understanding everything, first and foremost for the analyst and, subsequently, for the patient.

Furthermore, the patient is frequently unable to accept the interpretation, because this would entail admitting that it is not his creation, that the interpretation is created by the analyst. This situation brings us back to the denial of the most painful aspect of primal scene, that of the conception, because it confronts the subject with the hypothesis of his own inexistence. This can lead to the pure and simple elimination of the analyst and his interpretations when the patient, confronted with the birth of something new, portrays himself as having to run the risk of inexistence: 'What would have become of me without analysis?' This question then leads to another: 'What would have become of me if my parents had never met?'

Contrariwise, once the patient is able, symbolically, to recognize a certain matrix, i.e. that it is from the union of his words and the analyst's listening that the interpretation is 'born', the narcissistic dimension is overcome and at that point we may speak of an Oedipal position. Furthermore, death anxiety, 'nameless terror' (in the sense given by Bion (1962b) and Winnicott (1974)) in its non-representable nature, or in its representation as emptiness, can be masked, precisely by what is most specific in psychoanalysis: Language.

Indeed, *language may be narcissistically reappropriated* to conceal such anxiety. Certain tautological-narcissistic discourses, certain puns, certain metaphors in which the subject is not implicated can conceal the anxiety by which the subject feels threatened. The same may happen to the analyst: Certain interpretations are provoked by a 'nameless anxiety' that induces the analyst to speak. We should draw a sharp distinction with those interpretations aimed at recognizing that the analyst, functioning as a *witness*, has clearly heard the patient's anxiety (I am thinking, in particular, of Winnicott (1974)). In this way, the interpretation prevents anxiety from becoming psychic death through repetition.

In view of these propositions, it is to my mind evident that neither words nor silence are in themselves and exclusively the key to interpretative efficiency. I believe a certain *dilemma between silence and interpretation could be reformulated in this light.*

The fate of the analyst's interpretations

The analyst decides to remain silent or to interpret. The patient hears that the analyst's *silence is speaking to him*. He listens to the analyst's silence or interpretations and *reinterprets* them according to the history that contributed to the constitution of his psyche. As we shall see in the clinical example to follow, the analyst's interpretations are reinterpreted by the patient on the basis of a certain form of identification. Our analytic listening must allow us to grasp the way in which the analysand listens to our interpretations.

The analysand's discourse *reveals the identification*. When the identification ceases to be silent, the reinterpretation that the patient makes of the analyst's interpretations may also become audible. By means of such identifications, the patient's psyche makes links with what I have called the internal parents, in a repetitive and silent manner: He forms a narcissistic couple with each parent. At this juncture, I should like to put forward the following thesis: *The interpretations which the patient makes of the analyst's silence or interpretations will give a retroactive meaning* (après-coup) *to the discourse contained in the silence or in the interpretation.*

The analyst's presence manifests itself in 'listening to [the patient's] listening' (to the analyst's silence or interpretations). In this way every silence and every interpretation is over-signified. Paradoxically, a reinterpretation, which on one level might be considered as an 'obstacle' to listening to the interpretation, actually helps us to know *what it is we have said, over and above what we believe we have said*. This paradox will provide an essential understanding of my approach.

This brings us back to the important point of knowing whether one can talk about the analyst's presence, or function, without necessarily believing in a totally adequate object. To take into account, therefore, the way in which the patient hears the interpretations seems to me a particularly favourable moment for grasping the nature of these forms of resistance. The analyst's presence is thus linked to the listening to the listening function and not to the implicit supposition of a totally adequate object.

A difficulty in the path of psychoanalysis: The transmission of the analytic experience

We might ask ourselves whether it is possible to convey what the *clinical* situation leads us to anticipate, as answers to theoretical questions that are not yet clearly defined. Clinical experience imposes situations, often painful ones, in which the relevant questions are not always evident. How may we faithfully convey clinical situations dominated by nameless anxiety that can only be contained and worked through by the analyst in his countertransference?

Examples of interpretations in which the patient's response proves that a lifting of repression has taken place (thereby confirming the basic validity of the interpretation) do not allow me to eloquently illustrate what is at stake in this problem. I prefer to choose a session that could be considered as a 'failure' but in which the analytical process allowed both patient and analyst to *retroactively understand how the patient had listened to the interpretation together with the different aspects of narcissistic resistance at stake.*

During the analysis, and for a long time afterwards, failure itself proved to be meaningful for understanding both the patient's history (linked to her psychic constitution) and the transferential history. I shall present two fragments from two different sessions, separated by several years in the course of the analysis. The second session gave a retroactive meaning to the first. Between the two, the analytic working through had changed the analysand's psychic conditions of functioning, thereby allowing us to give new meaning to the first session.

Lise spent a large part of her sessions recounting anecdotes concerning the ill treatment and misfortune to which she was exposed. Situations were reified. The patient did not present herself as a protagonist of her world. She portrayed the world as natural: The world *was*. She spoke in terms of a closed situation. The analyst could find no opening through which to call that world into question. It was a discourse marked by narcissistic characteristics.

When Lise stopped relating anecdotes, she could not bear the silence and was unable to say what it was that inspired in her such anxiety, such nameless anxiety. We might say that when Lise *heard the analyst's silence*, the discourse implicit in the silence brought with it an anxiety that carried no associations. The only thing that could temper the catastrophic nature of this anxiety was the analyst's voice, which Lise heard as meaning that the analyst was alive so that she could feel that she, too, was psychically alive.

One difficult recurring theme concerned her father, whom she blamed for the unhappiness he caused whenever he was present (which was not very often). But the patient made a point of trying to get close to him in a way that was perhaps provocative. This always ended in conflict, with Lise feeling very unhappy. 'That's just the way father is', she said. Nevertheless, Lise always complained of his absence and sought to be with him whenever possible.

I formulated an interpretation in which I tried to establish a link between these situations, endeavouring to find a relationship between her unhappiness and an intrapsychic conflict. My implicit aim was to help the patient and myself to ask who in the transference was this analyst who listened to the analysand's complaints about her father. But my interpretation failed. The interpretation was as follows: 'You can only talk to me about one possible father, who makes you unhappy, and yet you seek him out.' The patient responded with a silence that, little by little, became transformed into an anxiety so great that it became catastrophic. She was unable, during the session, or at subsequent sessions, to say what caused such anxiety.

It required some years before she was able to speak about the session in these terms:

Do you remember that session when you said that I could only speak of my father *when* he made me unhappy? I understand now that I thought you were saying to me: 'Let go of your father, *because* he only makes you unhappy.' It was as though my mother had won again. I felt desperate because I could not say how she had won.

The original interpretation, it should be noted, was: 'You can only talk to me about one possible father, who makes you unhappy, and *yet* you seek him out.' So there are *three versions* of the interpretation: The one I actually said, what the patient understood and what she remembered as being my original interpretation. In fact, this 'remembered' version *was created by her* and *would* have been a better formulation of what I wanted to say.

Let us now consider the work of reconstructing Lise's history, which we carried out during the years that elapsed between the first and the second session. Many condensed and contradictory meanings attaching to her history had been touched on by my interpretation. First, although physically present, the father had been absent from the analysand's psychic universe since her birth. Her mother claimed that the father had never reconciled himself to the fact that a girl had been born and not a boy. Thus the analysand unconsciously believed that she had been doubly rejected: Through her mother (who was not loved by the father) and in herself, for what she herself was. The father took no interest in his daughter and she, in turn, believed that because of her 'error' in being a girl the couple formed by her parents was unable to be 'mended'.

Recalling my hypothesis that the patient speaks and listens according to a particular form of identification we understand that, when disidentification occurs, the patient's way of listening to the interpretation changes. I believe, retrospectively, that the working through of Lise's unconscious identification with her mother's way of functioning allowed her to begin the process of disidentification. *The interpretation heard through her identification with the mother* could begin to be compared by her with *another text*, which was her own creation. This brings us to a point that is crucial. Insofar as the key moment (which allows for transformation) is Lise's disidentification with her mother's psychic mode of functioning, it is necessary for us to explore further this particular mode.

The discourse of this kind of mother disregarded the logic of 'either–or'. It was a kind of functioning characteristic of the primary process (Freud 1911). All arguments, even the most incompatible ones, had the effect of depriving Lise of her father. This discourse, when governed by a particular logic characteristic of the primary process, I refer to as the *logic of the copper kettle*. I employ this metaphor with reference to Freud's example of how the unconscious process works. Let us recall the copper kettle joke:

A. borrowed a copper kettle from B. and after he had returned it was sued by B. because the kettle now had a big hole in it which made it unusable. His defence was:'First, I never borrowed a kettle from B. at all; secondly, the kettle had a hole in it already when I got it from him; and thirdly, I gave him back the kettle undamaged.'

(Freud 1905c: 62)

Freud comments:

[This] is an excellent example of the purely comic effect of giving free play to the unconscious mode of thought [. . .] This mutual cancelling-out by several thoughts, each of which is in itself valid, is precisely what does not occur in the unconscious. [. . .] there is accordingly no such thing as an 'either–or', only a simultaneous juxtaposition.

(ibid.)

Lise was unconsciously identified with the 'copper kettle logic' of her mother's discourse, which ignored 'either–or'. And when disidentification began, we understood that she had been listening to my interpretation as though it were based on 'copper kettle logic', using incompatible arguments to *deprive her of her father*, as her mother had done. This 'copper kettle logic' was in the service of the narcissistic logic. I said that my interpretation had failed. Now I am better able to understand that the failure partially depended on the way I had formulated this interpretation. I had myself spoken unawares in a style very close to the mother's discourse.

We shall analyse the 'copper kettle logic' from the point of view of the mother's discourse; from the point of view of my formulation ('You can only talk to me about one possible father, who makes you unhappy, and *yet* you seek him out'); and from the point of view of Lise's reinterpretation ('Let go of your father, *because* he only makes you unhappy').

In the *mother's* 'copper kettle logic', I was able to distinguish three aspects. First, it contained incompatible arguments that led the daughter to place herself constantly in unhappy situations corresponding in fact to the *mother's* psychic reality. Second, her words were equivalent to deeds whereby the girl's fate was already determined. The patient consequently did not believe that the words could mean anything other than what had already been 'said' once and forever (by the mother and, as we shall see, by the analyst in the transference). Third, this discourse was not easily perceptible in the patient's words, neither was it made explicit as a conflict during the sessions.

Reflecting on *the style of my interpretation*, we realize that I used not only the word 'yet', which was already a mistake, but also the expression 'you seek him out'. Words are equal to deeds. In the interpretation, I refer to an action. If to this we add that I say 'yet', the interpretation may imply 'stop looking for him'. The interpretation was reinterpreted by the patient in an imperative mode:You must let go of your father! Moreover, the interpretation begins with 'You can

27

only speak to me of': This spontaneous expression might have opened a third 'space' in which to ask *who* was the analyst in the transference, before whom 'one could only speak of'. But, the word 'only' (used in my interpretation) also converges with the other aspects of my formulation to *deprive* the patient of the *only* way she has to speak of her father and *anticipates* a modality that is not yet hers. It was better to have this father than to have none. The interpretation has, in its style, a narcissistic modality where the functions of appropriation and intrusion are considerably active.

In this sense, maybe we could say that there is an implicit interpretation in the transference: 'If you can "only speak to me of a unique possible father who makes you unhappy", you will not succeed in obtaining my love [implying that I, as your analyst, expect another kind of discourse].'

From the point of view of the *patient's listening to the interpretation*, it seems to me that, encouraged by my interpretative style, Lise heard in my interpretation *all* the arguments contained in the copper kettle's discourse in order to oust the father. Words are equal to deeds, as though the analyst were saying 'Stop suffering, let go of your father!' She might have imagined the analyst going so far as to use psychoanalytical arguments *with the sole object of depriving her of her father*. For example, with reference to the theory of masochism: 'Don't be masochistic, let go of your father.' Words said no more than what had *already* been 'said' once and forever. The words impel the patient to place herself in unhappy situations that correspond to the psychic reality of the mother. The interpretation is heard as an inexorable repetition: 'Your father is absent yet again.'

If we think now in terms of the function of 'listening to listening', we can say that I had been able to listen to the catastrophic anxiety with which the patient responded to my interpretation. Now I understand that the patient felt radically dispossessed, not only of the link with her father, but perhaps also, as a result, dispossessed of any link with me, as analyst. We might say that in this case the interpretation failed in its attempt to go beyond repetition in the transference; it also failed in its effort to include the father and, symbolically, the analyst. So *who* was I, the analyst, in the transference during that first particular session? What kind of transference prompted the catastrophic anxiety?

The question could only be answered *après-coup* when the patient could *say how she had heard my interpretation*. Both the interpretation and the transference now take on a retroactive meaning. From what has been said we can also realize that in the transference the analyst *is* the mother. Not just any mother, but *this particular mother*. How then may we maintain our analytical function and how may we interpret and overcome the narcissistic circuits present in the patient's discourse?

In the third version created by the patient and addressed to the analyst ('Do you remember that session when you said that I could only speak of my father when he made me unhappy?'), let us note that she begins by addressing me ('Do you remember that . . . you said that . . . I realize that I understood that'). The analyst's interpretation, thus, ceases to be identified by the patient as the mother's discourse. The interpretation is accepted as a discourse that *renders this father accessible. She has now another possible father* (and another possible language) for her psychic reality. This new father is a father *whom she cannot talk about in front of her mother.* Or perhaps it would be more accurate to say could not talk about in her mother's presence. In my view, 'when' designates oedipal rivalry with the mother (and with the analyst).

Now Lise can situate herself *vis-à-vis* both the interpretation and the reinterpretation, mediated by 'when' (which was already a part of her own personal language): She is speaking therefore of her transferential history.

In my understanding, the appearance of a conception of time in which the patient situates herself in relation to different moments of her history (included in the transferential history) best characterizes the 'depressive position' described by Melanie Klein.

Why has the identity of the analysand manifested itself in a narcissistic struggle, by which she would only listen to interpretations through maternal logic? The reason is, to my mind, that *her psychic reality was constituted at that moment in the analysis by this internal mother in relation to this internal father and that all of her, her entire identity, her being, was equivalent to this relationship.* We may recall in what sense I consider such discourses as narcissistic. They are narcissistic in that the self-love of each internal parent nourishes itself and takes for itself that which was worthy of love, even if it comes from the daughter (thus depriving her of a language of her own as well) and in rejecting into the daughter that which each of them hate in themselves: This process, where the functions of appropriation and intrusion are at stake, became evident in the transference. For example, the patient was afraid to show that she was doing better, because she thought she would be dispossessed of this experience by the analyst. Unconsciously, she fantasized that the analyst interpreted only for her own narcissistic glory and not with the aim of allowing the patient to make use of that which the interpretation revealed.

The disidentification can only take place when analyst and patient are able to recognize that *the patient's listening to the interpretation is linked to the internal parents, to their narcissistic discourses. Overcoming the narcissistic way of functioning* appears, thus, as the key concept for studying the *recognition of otherness*.

Retroactively, it might be said that I approached the clinical material according to three perspectives: The first is centred on the patient's narcissism; the second on the analyst's interpretation (caught by the narcissistic discourse of the patient's internal parents); and the third is centred on the transference. *Each of these perspectives thereby allows us to reveal what the other two hide*: Essentially the *not-me*, what is rejected by each ego in the light of these perspectives. From this particular point of view, I place the countertransference at the crossing of the analyst's narcissism, on the one hand, and the patient's narcissism, on the other (which includes, as we have seen, the internal parents' narcissism).

The active restitution of the analytic dissymmetry is achieved through the restitution of the transference contained in the countertransference: This constitutes a task of working through on the part of the analyst. It must be noted that the concepts of projection and of projective identification that constitute an element of this analysis, are part of a *larger* network that we are in the process of sketching out.

To resume, let us return to my initial thesis. The narcissistic resistances that create the most powerful obstacle to the psychoanalytical process are those stemming from the determination of the patient's identity, which in turn results from the narcissistic struggle with the internal parents that is repeated in the transference. A second thesis focuses on the analyst's function of listening to the patient's listening, which makes possible the analysis of the patient's narcissistic reinterpretations. What I find most interesting here is the creative fate of the interpretation (which constitutes the oedipal level). The analyst focuses his attention on the fate of his interpretation or on the fate of his silence in the patient's psyche. This is what I understand by 'the presence of the analyst': To listen and to interpret the destiny of what the patient has heard.

I hope that I have succeeded in demonstrating convincingly that the analysis of such resistances is possible without shortcircuiting the *discourse* of the patient or that of the analyst and that the analysis of these *resistances is not reductionistic, neither is it locked into a duality without history.*

Someone resists who is neither unique nor univocal (clinical experience is eloquent in this respect). It is precisely from the analysis of these resistances that a history is constructed. *The resistances themselves have a history as well.* I consider that this conjunction of resistances constitutes the 'narcissistic dimension of the Oedipus' (*le temps narcissique de l'Oedipe*). We might also question whether the analysis of resistances is necessary without 'errors' on the part of the analyst. Regarding the narcissistic resistances that have remained silent, we might ask whether these could not be resolved by themselves without our needing to analyse them? Furthermore, if we admit that it is legitimate to analyse narcissistic resistances, as I believe it is (including those of the analyst),[3] then we must redefine what a 'successful' session is. The question remains open.

The decision that the analyst takes to remain silent when faced with the narcissistic desire of the patient to make him speak, the decision to interpret over the narcissistic desire of the patient to make him remain silent, the choice of an interpretative content over the content that a discourse determined by the patient might impose, makes the analyst distinct from the patient and from the patient's narcissistic regulation. The way in which the patient considers the interpretations reveals the fate of this relationship.

We should not forget that in the *narcissistic relation the fate of the loved object is to lose its otherness.* The overcoming of the narcissistic relation implies that *hate* has ceased to be the only way in which the patient recognizes the other as such and differentiates himself from the other: Thus *love as well can sustain otherness.*

REPETITION AND SURPRISE: CONSTRUCTION AND ITS VALIDATION (1989)★

written with Antoine Corel★★

Introduction

We shall attempt to ascertain the conditions under which construction in psychoanalysis may be considered valid, i.e. those conditions that ensure that the construction truly corresponds to conflicts in the patient's own psyche and is not a theory 'constructed' by the analyst and inserted from outside the movement of the transference. We shall also try to demonstrate, using a clinical example, the importance of construction as a means of helping the patient to overcome an 'impasse' situation in his analysis.

The main hypothesis we shall develop is that the concept of construction, in its very structure, implies a very fertile paradox: Being by definition *retroactive*, it is at the same time *anticipatory*, in the sense that it establishes a precondition for access to psychical truths. We refer to the concept of *Nachträglichkeit*, translated by Strachey in the Standard Edition as 'deferred action' and in French as *après-coup*. For our purpose, we shall not draw a sharp distinction between reconstruction and construction. We shall thus be following Freud's usage, according to which the two terms are interchangeable, and we shall try to develop what in our view is a fruitful ambiguity between the two terms. We shall not comment on the extensive bibliography on this subject; let us only recall a few of the more recent contributions.

★ Presented at the International Psychoanalytical Congress, Rome, July 1989.
★★ Antoine Corel, MD, is a member of the Paris Psychoanalytical Society and of the Argentine Psychoanalytic Association (IPA). He is in private practice in Paris.

In 1979 in the 31st International Psychoanalytical Congress, New York, Harold Blum and Eric Brenman presented papers on 'The value of reconstruction in adult psychoanalysis' (see Blum 1980; Brenman 1980). Blum considers that reconstruction does not always automatically follow from transference and analytic work. It is an inferential and integrative act that restores the continuity and cohesion of the personality. He considers that what is reconstructed is not the historical event of a trauma, but the intrapsychic meaning of the experience. For his part, Brenman says that reconstructions are of therapeutic value only through the analysis of the repetition compulsion in the transference. He considers that new developments in the course of treatment need to be integrated with the creative constructions of the past, thus forming the foundations of new constructions.

We, for our part, endorse Blum's view that the main focus of interest is the intrapsychic meaning of experience. However, we would add that this meaning is to be found in the transferential movement. To pinpoint our position in relation to Blum and Brenman, we would refer to the different ideas contained in the analytic literature dealing with transference, but this would fall outside the scope of this essay.

In 1988 in Stockholm, the European Psychoanalytical Federation held a meeting on 'Construction and reconstruction in psychoanalysis'. Wolfgang Loch considered that constructions are always interpretations on the part of the analyst and that in fact there is no possibility of knowing the events of the patient's past; therefore, in his view, it is always a question of *construction* and never of *reconstruction*. Francis Pasche insisted that it is necessary, and even ethically imperative, to be sure that the analyst reconstructs the past. He said that *factual* events can be recognized as such during the course of psychoanalysis and can be the object of a reconstruction.

In his role as discussant in the First Plenary Discussion at that meeting, Joseph Sandler, referring to a previous paper (Sandler and Sandler 1987), said that as analysts we are confronted with a present unconscious that derives, but in ways that are probably unknowable, from an essentially unknowable past unconscious. He considered that in some cases constructions are disguised as reconstructions; he said that in the French literature references abound to reconstruction of primal scenes that are regarded, in his opinion, as real experiences.

In introducing the Final Plenary Discussion at Stockholm, Haydée Faimberg pointed out that the dilemma between construction and reconstruction expresses the analyst's concern to ensure that the (re)construction is *not* the outcome of *a narcissistic battle* to impose a truth on the other. In order to ensure that there is not an intrusion on the part of the analyst, some analysts prefer to speak of reconstruction in order to indicate that there is indeed a prior text, a mental referent guaranteeing that the object of reconstruction comes from the patient's mind. Other analysts, still with the same aim, prefer nevertheless to talk of construction because there is no proof, they say, that this prior text exists.

Loch, however, said that 'man is a being who interprets' and that 'there is no reality which has not already been an interpretation'. This means, he said, that interpretation, which is unavoidable, is bound to be an intrusion and that it *cannot not* be an intrusion.

In our essay, we will attempt to discover a way of overcoming the radical opposition between reconstruction and construction. Since the danger of the possible intrusion of the analyst's theoretical preconceptions is central to the debate, we shall set out the conditions that, in our opinion, have to exist for the (re)construction to be valid.

Narcissistic resistance and early history

We would like to begin by recalling Freud's assertion that construction consists in exposing to the patient 'a piece of his early history that he has forgotten' (Freud 1937: 261). Our basic assumption is that this 'early history' is actualized in the transference. To support our argument, we shall examine this actualization at that particular moment in the transference process *when narcissistic resistance appears*.

Although this paper is centred on the problem of construction, we must mention some complementary hypotheses previously developed by one of us. Our reasoning is based on a view of narcissism compatible with Freud's works of 1914–15. We do not therefore consider either the concept of ego in the second structural theory or the differentiation between ego and self. This does not imply any judgement in regard to these concepts: We are merely postponing a study of narcissism with reference to the different psychoanalytical schools. On the one hand, some authors centre their thinking on Freud's work (but we know there are different ways of reading Freud), others on post-Freudian authors. On the other hand, we are aware that some well-known studies of narcissism can only be compared with one another in the light of their theoretical context (ego psychology, self-psychology, the theory of object relations . . .). Even then, a school cannot be reduced to a homogeneous line of thought. And, last but not least, there are authors who establish links between the different schools.

In such a complex situation, if we had considered narcissism before examining what we meant by narcissistic resistance, we would have been obliged to go far beyond our scope. For this reason, we are not considering any writing on narcissism apart from Freud's (1914b).

To sum up: We take a perspective linked to a *single* period of Freud's work (1914–15). We are viewing narcissism *only* as a resistance, that is, in the clinical situation. We know that Freud did not refer to 'narcissistic resistance' in the clinical situation (although he was the first to mention it in 1917 as an epis-temological resistance, as we saw in Chapter 2) or to the 'narcissistic dimension of the Oedipal configuration' (which is a central concept in our study).

33

In the transference process, narcissistic resistance is brought into play in order to avoid any revelation from the unconscious which might threaten this illusion of omnipotence and to prevent the emergence of the three painful aspects of the oedipal situation: Recognition of the difference between generations, of the difference between sexes and of otherness. These three kinds of resistance form *the narcissistic dimension of the Oedipal configuration.*

We deal exclusively with the resistance shown to recognizing the difference between generations *as made apparent in a construction.* Moreover, the narcissistic resistance to acknowledging the difference between generations is, as we shall see, discovered at the same time as a particular type of unconscious identification (which is actually at the root of the resistance itself). Our clinical example shows that this special type of unconscious identification involves a 'telescoping of generations'.

Surprise in the transference

Jacques is in his fourth year of analysis. He is a writer of great creative ability who first came to analysis in order to resolve problems of inhibition in his work and because he intensely hated the people he loved most. The psychic changes achieved as a result of the working through of his psychic conflicts were materialized in the following way: He began to write again, he got married and, at the time the session we describe here took place, he had been a father for one year. When these changes began to occur, the patient fell prey to cycles of catastrophic anxiety that lacked any psychic representation. At times, he was seized by despair and hate, which caused him to twist his body on the couch and to beat against the wall. The situation was a source of preoccupation for the analyst because, although interpretation succeeded in relieving the anxiety within each session, the repetition of these bursts of anxiety without representation still persisted. The anxiety attacks experienced by the patient were undermining the progress he was achieving in the working through of his psychic conflicts, with the resumption of his writing and with the changes in his personal life.

This particular session began with the patient evoking a scene from his childhood, which he had already mentioned many times in the course of his analysis and which concerned the patient's erotic curiosity about his mother's body. In previous sessions, the memory had always resisted any association, but this time the scene was associated with a dream:

> I had a dream last night, of an extraordinary lunar landscape. Time had stopped. I was filled with a feeling of strangeness. From a kind of cave, there emerged a person – that person was me yet again it was not me. I looked at him, this very weird man, who was made up of a number of fragments which seemed to have been sewn together. The surroundings were those of a lunar

landscape, which were familiar to me, yet unfamiliar. Strange, but already known.

You know, it makes me think now of a Russian landscape – which I know nothing about, never having been to Russia – but my father and my grandfather must have been familiar with it, both of them being Russian. [Here, Jacques falls silent for a time.]

My father was the youngest child in a large, very poor Jewish family. My grandfather had decided right from my father's birth that he would be a labourer. Only the eldest son was entitled to study. You know, in Russia, the Jews were really poor, and didn't have many opportunities. [Silence once again.]

You know, it's only right now that I realize that the thing I've always reproached my father for, when I tell you he was going to swallow me . . . I don't mean he's going to swallow me . . . what I reproach him for . . . is that he's just a worker – that he is *nothing more* – that he never tried to become somebody, to raise himself up.

In this sequence, the following points seem worthy of our attention. First, the erotic curiosity about the mother is for the first time associated with Jacques' father. Second, Jacques' father appears as the husband of his wife for the first time, and, more importantly, as the son of the analysand's grandfather. This is also a first-time association. Until this session, Jacques' father had persistently appeared, during the sessions of the preceding year, as a mirror image of a voracious mouth demanding to be fed. For instance, once, at a restaurant, Jacques thought: 'Now he's going to demand that I pay for everything he eats.' This idea had imposed itself on Jacques' mind even if the father really demanded nothing. Quite the contrary, he was at that time helping him to purchase an apartment. Still the voracious mouth persisted in Jacques' fantasies and reappeared in the transference: The analyst was going to devour everything the analysand could achieve . . . in analysis.

As she listened to the patient's description of the dream, the analyst was very surprised by the patient's unprecedented association, with his grandfather and with the grandfather–father relationship. She thought that this association revealed something very important and deeply felt. She noticed that the patient, too, was very much surprised by his *own* realization and that the association seemed to carry a strong affective element. Indeed, the association was experienced as a surprise by *both* the patient and his analyst. This shared experience stimulated a lively curiosity in both of them.

The analyst (approximately) said:

You feel like a man who has been made up of different pieces originating from different places and times – a man who has been born to a situation that is old and new at the same time. As you feel that these fragments are not compatible with one another, you also feel that they require incompatible solutions. One fragment speaks to us about your father, who is also the younger-brother-condemned-not-to-study-by-his-own-father, and who therefore also condemns you in your mind, not to make progress in the pursuits that are so dear to you.

A few sessions later, the patient mentioned for the first time a famous writer, saying in the most casual way that this writer was his uncle. The analyst pointed out that the patient had spoken as though the analyst should already have known about this uncle. The patient reacted again with surprise at never having mentioned his uncle before since he was, as Jacques added, 'my mother's great love; for her, he is the only one that counts'.

The surprise here is shared by the patient and the analyst. The former was familiar with the story, the latter was unaware of it. (In other cases, the analyst has actually been told of such fragments and subsequently forgotten them. Later in the analysis, what is important is that she remembers the fragments *with* the patient.)

We must now open a parenthesis. Paradoxical as it may seem, *certain conditions facilitate surprise* and one of these is that the analyst refrains from proposing a construction prematurely. A construction is premature if it does not respect the patient's words and is a deduction rooted exclusively in the analyst's theory. (Even if the 'construction' based on the analyst's own preconceptions coincides with what happened to the patient in the past, this construction could have the same effects as an interpretation out of context.) The danger of intruding with the construction is met at a previous stage by the analyst's stance of actively waiting and tolerating the anxiety of not knowing, which ensures the authenticity of what is going to be the object of the construction. We close our parenthesis.

We must admit that it is astonishing indeed that the patient could have been surprised by events that he had known of all along since it was (and *had* to be) he who ultimately revealed those events. In the following paragraphs, we shall attempt to trace the origin of the patient's feeling of surprise. In the session we are considering, as Jacques describes the appearance of his dream landscape – strange, Russian, at once familiar and unknown – he is struck by the associations that come into his mind. *The story acquires a new meaning for the patient: Both* he and his analyst are hearing *this* story for the first time.

Indeed, when the patient speaks and organizes the events so as to communicate them to his analyst, these events have already become a narrative in the patient's mind. This points to the *difference between information and history*. One indication of their non-equivalence is the patient's own surprise: Only in the process of telling does the unconscious link between his father's history *and* his own psychic structure begin to dawn on the patient.

Constructing a missing link

Although Jacques had always been aware of these events in his father's history, he had never realized that he had identified with them on an unconscious level. We must not be led astray by the fact that Jacques knew all the time about those events. The knowledge was of no use to him so long as he did not know that those events concerned him, so long as he had not worked through their meaning so as to integrate them as part of his own history. There was a *missing link* between those events and the way in which they concerned *him*.

Thus, he could only repeat the situation in his own destiny, in the transference and in his anxiety crises. Let us remember here what Freud wrote in 1914: 'The patient repeats instead of remembering . . . under the conditions of resistance' (Freud 1914a: 151) 'and in the end we understand that [repeating] is his way of remembering' (op. cit.: 150).

When finally he is able to dream, Jacques represents himself as being composed of heterogeneous fragments. Coming after the memory of his erotic curiosity about his mother's body and before the associations with his father's history, the dream enables the analyst to establish an *unprecedented link*, i.e. a construction, which relates the incompatible unconscious identifications to *that* particular image of the father.

This link is a logical one in the construction formulated by the analyst, similar to the logical link that Freud constructed in the second phase of the girl's fantasy in 'A child is being beaten':

> This second phase is the most important and the most momentous of all. But we may say of it in a certain sense that it *has never had a real existence. It is never remembered*, it has never succeeded in being conscious. It is a *construction of analysis, but it is no less a necessity* on that account.
>
> (Freud 1919a: 185 (emphasis added))

> [. . .] the second phase [. . .] is incomparably the more important. This is not only because it continues to operate through the agency of the phase that takes its place; we can also detect effects upon the character, which are directly derived from its unconscious form.
>
> (Freud 1919a: 195)

Freud's two papers read in conjunction help us to understand that *if the patient repeats instead of remembering, it is either because the representation has never existed or because it has not been integrated into his own psychic space. In both cases the analyst's construction provides a missing link.*

Let us once again ask ourselves what Freud meant when he said that 'construction consists in exposing to the patient a piece of his early history that he has forgotten'. In our view, he meant that construction provides a new and unprecedented link whereby the past is constituted as such and the patient acquires a history, his history. We propose, now, to examine this link.

The father–brother

In *Totem and Taboo* (Freud 1912–13), Freud says that a fraternal alliance is necessary for the establishment of the father's image. In this case, the father was not considered as such but as a brother. The difference of generations was blurred (telescoping of generations) and the father was considered as a sibling: A *father–brother*. Instead of a real *oedipal rivalry*, we have a *narcissistic* struggle between siblings. This is what we call the *narcissistic dimension of the Oedipal configuration*. In the analysis this gives rise to intense resistance; for want of a father image, the patient clings to this narcissistic version of the oedipal conflict as it is felt to be essential for the structuring of his psyche. In this case, the subversion of the oedipal rivalry – a rivalry with a father–brother – was only in part linked to the father's history in the patient's psyche. There is another factor that came up some sessions later with the mention of the uncle, the writer, 'my mother's great love'. The mother's desire for her brother and Jacques' desire for his mother *merged effectively to exclude* the father from the patient's psyche.

This material provides us with the means of understanding that Jacques, as a writer, was following the destiny of his uncle, idealized as a love object by the patient's mother and having become the patient's own ego ideal. This is how Jacques' father came to be condemned in the patient's fantasies to being unloved by the patient's mother (not being entitled to the love she bestowed on her intellectual brother) and condemned by the grandfather never to acquire culture.

The entire situation had suffered drastic condensation in the patient's mind. One of the patient's unconscious fantasies (which served the function of resisting narcissistically the oedipal wound) can be summed up as follows:

> How can I hate my father, and how can I enter into rivalry with him as such, when he is just a poor young son, condemned by his own father never to study? Besides my grandfather, a poor Russian Jew, had nothing to say about his own destiny either.

Likewise, we became aware of an enigmatic and contradictory complaint. Sometimes, Jacques said that he had come into the world too early and sometimes, too late. When he said 'too early' he was expressing the fantasy, due to his having been conceived shortly after the marriage, that he 'completed' his mother and excluded the father. At other times, in spite of being the eldest son, he felt that he had come too late: 'It's no use for me to go on writing, it has all been said before. I came into this world too late.' It is now clear to us that in saying 'too late' he was speaking for his father and that this is the precise juncture at which identification occurred (too late in the family, too late to win the love of his wife).

Repetition and narcissistic resistance

It is not difficult to understand how, as a result of this extreme condensation of his early history, Jacques is compelled to express his contradictory desires in a very explosive way. Although previous interpretations had provided the possibility of a partial working through of the conflict, Jacques would still come to his next session filled with an anxiety of catastrophic proportions, devoid of representation. He was also subject to bursts of hatred for everyone whom he loved most. In the transference, this expression took the form of anxiety and hatred. This hatred was the means by which he differentiated himself from others. In other words, the patient's early history always led him back to a *new cycle of repetition*. In the circumstances, the different interpretations converge to form a 'navel', which provides the basis for the construction.

Once the construction has been provided by the analyst, we *are able to understand retroactively (nachträglich) both the father's history and the patient's narcissistic resistance*. But the fact that the father's history finds expression in the patient's narcissistic resistance would indicate that this *narcissistic resistance has a history of its own* and that it was *this* resistance that had prevented the patient all along from working through the interpretations.

We are thus led retroactively to formulate a question that should logically have been asked before the construction was established. *Who* resists the analyst's interpretations? It is Jacques – *identified with the father–brother* – who resists the interpretations because Jacques, the eldest son, is in conflict with the father, the younger son, condemned-by-the-father-not-to-study. Thus we can trace the origin of this resistance back to the *incompatibility* of fragments, which, in turn, naturally implies incompatible solutions. This incompatibility is radical because it concerns Jacques' narcissistic identity and we think, to repeat ourselves, that it explains at least partially the catastrophic anxiety.

The interpretations that the analyst had formulated in accordance with a modality of oedipal rivalry *were reinterpreted by Jacques in accordance with a modality of narcissistic struggle*, as between brothers (narcissistic dimension of the Oedipal configuration). Thus the revelation of unconscious identifications through construction enables the analyst to gain a retroactive understanding of how the patient has understood the interpretations. The analyst obtains the means to understand, retroactively, the value and the limits of his interpretations.

A fertile paradox

Now we are able to explore our hypothesis that the concept of construction, in its very structure, implies a very fertile paradox: Being by definition retroactive, it is at the same time anticipatory, in the sense that it establishes a precondition for access to psychical truths. Thus, retroactively, we found in our clinical example a particular type of identification that enabled us to grasp the *cause* of the resistance, the *history of the resistances*.

Construction provided a *retroactive* meaning for that which had previously existed in the form of repetitive anxiety. (This also means differentiating between the concepts of resistance and of defence. We consider that resistance is an eminently clinical concept, present in the transferential process and acting in opposition to analytic work.)

With reference now to the *anticipatory* movement, let us recall what Freud says.

> For the archaeologist the reconstruction is the aim and end of his endeavours while for analysis the construction is only a *preliminary* labour.
>
> (Freud 1937: 260 (emphasis added))

In this sense we may consider that construction has opened up the possibility of access to psychic truths, i.e. it has become a precondition for such access. We prefer to call this 'preliminary labour' anticipatory movement, to show that there is already in the present a trend towards the future: The construction provides access to new material (in our example, the mother's incestuous desire for her writer brother).

Construction and its validation

Of the problems created by the relationship between material reality and its psychic inscription, we have retained only the concept of *psychic truths* (see Chapter 8), considered for our purposes here only from the point of view of the narcissistic adherence by the patient to a certain version of this story, which is a constituent part of his own identity. This narcissistic version is not unique, and it may change; therefore we prefer to speak of psychic truths.[1]

Besides, we think that construction, which originates in the junction of the material springing from the unconscious and the interpretive activity of the analyst, coincides in its *inner logic* with the movement of the analytic process and with the working of the psyche. It remains now for us to speak of the criteria for validating the construction.

For Freud:

[T]he path that starts from the analyst's construction . . . does not always lead so far [i.e. to the patient's recollection]. Quite often we do not succeed in bringing the patient to recollect what has been repressed. Instead of that, if the analysis is carried out correctly, we produce in him an assured *conviction of the truth of the construction* which achieves the same therapeutic result *as a recaptured memory*.

(Freud 1937: 265–6 (emphasis added))

All our reasoning leads us *not* to expect the construction to be confirmed by a memory as a sign of the lifting of repression. We have pointed out that there is nothing to remember, that it is not a matter of filling gaps in the memory. Rather, as we have seen, it is a question of proposing a link that has never existed. The 'conviction of the truth' referred to by Freud has been implicitly present throughout this paper:

1   In the surprise shared by patient and analyst at what came to light and the resulting construction.
2   In the retroactive understanding of the repetition.
3   In the access to new versions of psychic truths.

In general, we may say that the construction is validated by the discontinuation of repetition and by the appearance of new material.

To conclude, we have established the difference between information and historicity. Our development, in the light of our clinical example, of Freud's definition, has enabled us to qualify what he implied by the patient's 'forgetting': Rescuing a fragment of early 'history' and thus breaking the cycle of its repetition in the transference implies for us that *construction precisely transforms into history* that which had previously existed *not as a memory, but only as repetition*.

4

THE COUNTERTRANSFERENCE POSITION AND THE COUNTERTRANSFERENCE (1989)*

I shall refer in this essay to the psychical activity of the analyst during the session, for which I shall put forward the concept of the countertransference position. I would not use a neologism if I did not consider it more appropriate to the problems raised by the countertransference as I see them at present. After all, the countertransference has been discussed in a wide range of contexts and is not *an unequivocal concept*. I shall not offer a historical review of the concept or an enumeration of the bibliographical references, but shall confine myself to some aspects essential for an understanding of my argument. The term 'counter-transference' may denote not only the unresolved neurotic aspects of the analyst but also his unconscious psychical functioning.

Annie Reich and Margaret Little were among the first analysts to use the concept of countertransference, but their respective positions were always very different: Annie Reich reserves the term exclusively for the analyst's unresolved *neurotic* aspects and affirms in an extremely polemical tone that its semantic field must not be widened, whereas Margaret Little sets out to show that the *impersonal analyst is a myth*. Heinrich Racker explicitly takes this second position as his starting point. This polemic has so divided the analytical world that the use of the concept of countertransference inevitably suggests neurosis and *misunderstandings therefore arise if the term is employed in a wider sense*.

Heinrich Racker read his paper 'Neurosis of countertransference' to the Argentine Psychoanalytic Association in 1948. Using different clinical examples, he showed that the oedipal structure of the analyst and the way he resolves his

---

* A slightly abridged version of this text was presented at the Paris Psychoanalytical Society's Grenoble Colloquium 'Questions for Tomorrow' on 19 November 1989. This text is the published complete version (1992).

direct and reverse Oedipus complex may condition his acceptance of what the patient says. Racker did not publish this study until 1952 because his colleagues felt it unwise to imply that an analyst might be subject to the effects of his own neurosis. In his subsequent work, Racker studied the analyst's psychical functioning in a way that dispensed with the concept of neurosis. As we know, Donald Winnicott wrote 'Hate in the counter-transference' in 1947, while Paula Heimann published her famous paper 'On countertransference' in 1950. I am in debt to Racker, Heimann and Winnicott, even if the concept of counter-transference I am putting forward has undergone a substantial transformation. I shall now consider the nature of this new viewpoint and attempt to justify my coinage of a neologism.

To begin with, I would point out that my fundamental choice has been to refer to the analyst's overall psychical activity, *placed in the service of listening to what the patient says or cannot say during the session.* This psychical activity centres on the analytic function and, to the extent that it is directed towards listening to the patient's discourse, their positions – the analyst's and the patient's – are dissymmetrical. Some conceptions of the countertransference, however, suggest an interchangeable, symmetrical position for the two protagonists. This is one of the three reasons why I speak of the analyst's position. The second reason is that the analyst gets his bearings in relation to his countertransference, while the third is that his way of getting his bearings implies that he analyses his countertransference as the *result* of a dialectical relationship between different factors. *The countertransference position is modified in turn by the very fact of analysing this dialectic.*

All the foregoing justifies the idea of a *position.* Why then do we not simply speak of the analyst's position? Since we are, in fact, concerned with the overall activity of the analyst, an activity intended to restore what corresponds to the *history of the transference*, it seems to me preferable to qualify it as pertaining to the countertransference. This term conforms first and foremost to the logic of analytic practice. In so far as we are concerned to open up a new prospect and not merely to give a new name to a concept (which is, in any case, not unequivocal), the coining of a neologism, rather than exacerbating the existing psychoanalytic Babel, has a clarifying effect.

To sum up, I define the countertransference position as all the psychical activity of the analyst intended to restore what corresponds to the history of the transference. This position depends on a dialectical causality.

I now turn to the possible *consequences* for analytic theory and practice of the *absence of the concept* of the countertransference or, as I am suggesting, of the countertransference position. Even if the analyst, for theoretical reasons, considers that the countertransference plays no part in the analytic treatment, he will nevertheless be situated in a countertransference position. In my opinion, such a theory will *lack a concept*, thus preventing the analyst from following the movements of his own psychical functioning during the patient's treatment and hence from modifying this functioning. As I see it, the outcome of this hypothetical case is that the analyst *will tend not to listen to anything stemming from the patient that threatens to arouse unpleasure in him.* Yet many *enigmas posed by the transference* are finally resolved because the analyst discovers the beginnings of unpleasure in his countertransference and follows this track that has been unexpectedly revealed.

Overcoming the resistances to hearing something that arouses unpleasure entails demanding psychical work on the part of patient and analyst alike. This study develops this hypothesis in both depth and breadth. (For the narcissistic resistances of the *analyst*, see Chapters 2 and 9.) This said, of the analysts who accept the idea of the countertransference in their publications, some embrace a more linear than dialectical conception of its psychical causality. In other cases, where the *dialectical* conception of this causality is respected, the term 'countertransference' is reserved for a particular moment of the causal nexus. I consider this approach to be perfectly legitimate, provided only that we define our terms precisely. For this purpose, I shall examine some of these views on the countertransference, on the basis of my broader conceptualization of the countertransference position. This will, I hope, allow me gradually to identify the factors involved in the dialectical determination of this position.

First of all, the countertransference position is *not* merely a matter of the *neurotic* conflicts of the analyst. These are the conflicts that the analyst has worked through in his own analysis and which he makes allowance for when they interfere with the analytic function. If reactivated, they do not necessarily prevent the analyst from taking other factors into account – whereas the neurotic aspect may precisely prevent him from recognizing the other factors involved. I shall elucidate this point later.

The countertransference position does *not* depend *only* on the patient's transference, although the latter plays an essential part. The countertransference position *cannot* be defined as the *patient's creation alone*. At this point, however, we must give due credit to Paula Heimann (1950) who, precisely because she considered that the countertransference was created by the patient, *overcame the ban on the use of the term 'countertransference' for anything other than the unresolved aspects of the analyst's neurosis*. Moreover, I think that the patient cannot create the analyst's response but only the *conditions* for the analyst to respond with his *own* psychical functioning. For instance, if we believe that what the analyst feels corresponds exactly, *without any mediation*, to what the patient feels, this will have both theoretical and practical consequences. However, this is not the right forum for discussing them.

The concept of the countertransference position is not something ineffable to which the analyst can resort in order to save himself the trouble of thinking about complex metapsychological problems. From this point of view, the debate can only be impoverished if the analyst uses his 'countertransference reactions' alone to discuss psychoanalytic problems, instead of taking the countertransference as a *point of departure* for the exploration of a more complex system. Hence the countertransference position in my sense *is not defined solely by the analyst's affect, although anxiety and affect are essential to its conception*. I shall discuss this problem later with reference to the countertransference symptom.

The countertransference position and the analyst's psychic presence

I have suggested that the psychical presence or absence of the analyst should be taken as an indicator of the countertransference position (Faimberg 1989a). Examination of this parameter may be interfered with by the polemics between analysts, who have frequently divided up the area of the debate into watertight – often ideological – compartments. Consideration of the status of the object in psychoanalysis and the concept of countertransference have substantially flowed from Lacan's critique of Balint's (1968) idea of the 'basic fault'.

The problem arising out of the historical antecedents of this polemic is that there is often *a failure to distinguish between the idea of the unsuitability of the object for satisfying the drive (hence the concept of a lack) and that of the analyst's psychical presence and absence*. I agree with the view that the object is unsuitable for completely satisfying the drive; in order to understand my argument it is important not to confuse the idea of the psychical presence of the analyst with that of the suitability of the object. Since the countertransference position depends on a large number of complex factors that are dialectically interrelated, we shall abandon the method of affirming what such a position is not and consider the factors that condition it in its positive aspects.

The first relevant factor is the *patient's discourse* – not only what he says but also what he does *not* say – that determines how the analyst listens to him. The patient's discourse arouses in the analyst a form of psychical functioning that he (the analyst) must analyse so as to distinguish what corresponds to the patient from what corresponds to himself. Here, of course, is the foundation of Freud's recommendation that the analyst should have been analysed himself. However, it seems plain to me that the analysis of the countertransference position will differ according to the analyst's personal characteristics, the relationship he had with his own analyst (which constitutes his own transference history) and the *theoretical* orientation he has espoused as a result, and in the service, of his practice.

The personal background will be just as important as the analytic filiation and I consider that the theoretical position has to do with both. As to the personal filiation, the analyst's personal characteristics may induce him to prefer one theoretical position to another because it fits in better with his *own* mode of psychical functioning. But the analyst's theoretical position is also bound up with his analytic filiation in so far as the latter results from what has been transmitted to him by his own analyst and supervisors. Of course, both the supervisors and the analyst's analyst are links in the chain of psychoanalytic transmission, in a manner of which the *protagonists are not always conscious.* We all know that the characteristics of the psychoanalytic movement differ according to geographical area. In France, Michel Neyraut (1974) advanced our under-standing of this problem by pointing out that, *in practice*, the countertransference anticipates the transference. Joyce McDougall (1989) emphasized the propensity of the countertransference to 'create new forms of thinking', as she herself put it, which help us to understand some patients' psychosomatic troubles.

The countertransference position as symptom

I had a patient who had the effect of inducing psychical absence in me: My mind would tend to wander during the sessions. When this situation recurred, I was forced to reflect on my countertransference position. I then analysed my personal constellation, identifying what corresponded to it and what aspects of it were being reactivated, possibly as a result of what the patient was saying or not saying. Next I made the provisional hypothesis that my *psychical absence was a counter-transference symptom*. The hypothesis of a symptom meant that I had to try to detect the terms of the conflict.

Alerted by the repetition of my psychical absence, I was able during a session to recognize in my countertransference an incipient unpleasant affect. Was my psychical absence a way of taking flight from this? I eventually concluded that the countertransference *symptom was the unpleasure itself*, which, concealed by my absence, might have passed unnoticed. By virtue of the analysis of my countertransference position, I moved from a position *of psychical absence to one of incipient anxiety*. The theoretical concept of the countertransference position has consequences in analytic practice: My psychical absence as an analyst during the session calls for an explanation. In this case it constituted a coun-tertransference symptom. The symptom could *not* be explained by postulating a *one-to-one correlation* between the psychical absence of the analyst and the psychical absence of the patient.

Here is an approximate reconstruction of a fragment of a session in which I realized that I was beginning to absent myself psychically: The patient was talking in a monotonous, barely audible and slightly contemptuous tone.

> *Analyst*: Let us listen to the way you have been speaking to me: In a monotonous voice, very quiet and hard to understand. That suggests to me that you do not think it very important to know whether I have heard you or not.
> *Patient*: At any rate, I often feel that you are not interested in me.

Analyst: Because you are talking to someone who you are convinced is not interested in what you say or what you are, you answer hopelessly and cease to take any interest in what you are telling us.

When I think about this fragment, I am inclined to say that, before any exchange was possible, we (the patient and myself) were in a *state of narcissistic self-sufficiency*, in this way concealing our despair at being unable to communicate. *It was precisely in the sense she most dreaded that the patient aroused psychical effects in me*, because the link on which her psychical relationship was based proved to be disinvested. In consequence the psychoanalytic process as a whole ran this risk. Analysis of my countertransference position enabled me to recognize the desinvestment of the analysis as a consequence of the unrecognized, and hence uninterpreted, narcissistic transference.

The countertransference position and the function of 'listening to listening'

The resources I deploy to break the vicious circle resulting from the psychical absence of the two protagonists are the concepts of: Narcissistic transference (which is discussed in Chapter 5); the countertransference position, which is our subject; and the function of 'listening to listening', which is worthy here of some brief comments. The analyst's psychical presence or absence is the result of the dialectic between what the patient says or does not say and what the analyst can hear on the basis of the highly complex personal equation outlined already. The idea of listening to listening gives priority to the analyst's countertransference position insofar as it emphasizes how the analyst listens again to his own interpretation as already interpreted by the patient. In order to do this, it is essential for the analyst to analyse his own countertransference position. It is my conviction that what the patient cannot say through parapraxes, dreams, silences and symptoms can only be heard from the countertransference position of the analyst.

In our example, by listening to the way the patient spoke, we were able to define her manner of relating as *a relationship with someone who was psychically absent*. My interpretation therefore centred on what the patient had said; her reply implied that I took no interest in what she *said* because I was not interested in what she *was*. In this sense, the patient accepted the content of the interpretation but *reinterpreted it in a different mode*: I interpreted on the level of saying and she responded on the level of being.

The countertransference position and the negative capability

Racker (1953) uses the term 'complementary identification' to denote the analyst's unconscious identification *with the object with which the patient identifies him*. The analyst can recognize this type of complementary identification to the extent that he analyses his countertransference position, by taking account of all the factors I have mentioned, including, of course, the analyst's theory. *The theoretical concept of complementary identification in turn contributes to recognition of the unconscious identification* and facilitates analysis of the analyst's countertransference position.

In 1934, before her own analytic training, Marion Milner drew attention to Keats' expression 'negative capability'. As we know, Bion took up this formulation in his celebrated contribution on memory and desire (Bion 1967). I myself consider that negative capability involves the acquisition of a new analytic capability in which the analyst places himself actively in the countertransference position of not knowing in order to be able to listen to, and be surprised by, the unknown. This presupposes that the analyst can contain the anxiety of not knowing and get his bearings in relation to what as yet has no representation. In other words, the analyst puts himself in the countertransference position of containing the unpleasure generated both by what the patient rejects of himself as unpleasant and by what is still an enigma. In a word, the analyst contains in his countertransference position an as yet unanalysed part of the transference.

If the analyst fails to contain the countertransference symptom and does not recognize it, he will tend in his turn to reject what arouses unpleasure in him and will probably decide that his patient is not analysable. This does not mean that every patient is analysable, but that analysability depends on *both* protagonists, patient and analyst, and not only on the patient. Precisely for this reason, analysis of the countertransference position has implications in the sphere of what I like to call psychoanalytic ethics. When we decide to accept a patient, one of the criteria we use is whether the suffering communicated (by words or by silence) to us by this individual patient can be contained by our counter-transference position. If we take a positive decision, we shall have helped to create the conditions whereby the unsayable can become sayable. The ethical aspect has to do with the fact that this decision calls for a precise analysis of our personal constellation, enabling us to evaluate our ability to place *our psychical functioning in the service of this specific patient*. When we decline to accept a patient, this may mean 'I cannot be your analyst' and not necessarily 'You are unanalysable'. It seems to me that the ethical aspect here is that, by acknowledging *our* limits, we are allowing the patient to look for the analyst who will best be able to help him. However, I must emphasize that this does not mean that every person must be deemed analysable.

I should like to mention the feelings aroused in me insistently by one of my patients, which converged in a countertransference position that I interpreted as one of *despair*. I had the good fortune to begin supervising this patient with José Bleger, who pointed out (at a time when these things were not talked about, in a personal communication in 1962) that the unconscious sense of guilt from which my patient was suffering at having survived the concentration camp in which his entire family had perished was, although he was unaware of it, preventing him from feeling that he *deserved* the analysis we were undertaking (see Modell 1965). Bleger's theoretical position helped me to modify my own countertransference position and, consequently, to detect the transference contained within the countertransference.

In conclusion, I would say that, as in Greek tragedy, some patients fulfil their destiny by creating an impossible analytic situation. Unravelling the ineluctable web of destiny entails recognizing, analysing and transforming the counter-transference position so as to reveal the extent of transference repetition deployed through the psychical functioning of the analyst. But we cannot unravel what we fail to recognize.

Perhaps the question *'What is my countertransference position?'* is often the only one that can help us answer the other question: *'Is this patient analysable?'*

The countertransference position is ultimately the meeting point of intrasubjectivity, intersubjectivity and metapsychology. That is why it is absolutely essential for us to examine our countertransference position if we are to overcome repetition and create something unprecedented.

5

THE NARCISSISTIC
DIMENSION OF THE OEDIPAL
CONFIGURATION (1993)*

Introduction

I have noticed time and again that patients associate to fragments of their parents' history in *response* to my interpretations related to their narcissistic functioning in the transference. Thus we come into contact with aspects of the patient's history that are intimately linked to the parents' history as *(re)constructed*. In other words, the patient's intrapsychic struggle is reconstructed in the transference in a fragmentary way and related to partial aspects of their parents' history. Should we regard the interweaving of both histories (the parents' and the child's) as just anecdotal or subsidiary? In different writings, I have been exploring answers to this question and I have arrived at the hypothesis that the *narcissistic modality discovered in the transference had also been partially transmitted by the parents*.

What is transmitted is not always a content but essentially a narcissistic way of solving the conflicts. This means that parents transmit to their child the narcissistic functioning they used to solve their intrapsychic conflicts, including the oedipal ones. A conflict of an oedipal nature can be 'solved' in a narcissistic modality.

The aim of this essay is to present the following hypothesis. In the working through of the oedipal conflict in each and every analysis we reach a moment of struggle against narcissistic figures. In this situation the subject feels that he totally possesses the object or he is totally excluded by the object: The patient functions with the logic of 'either–or'; let us call the product of this kind of logic a 'narcissistic dilemma'.

---

* This version was presented at the International Psychoanalytical Congress, Amsterdam, July 1993.

The overcoming of this narcissistic dilemma (re-enacted in the transference) constitutes a momentous step in the analysis of the oedipal conflict. *I propose to conceptualize this narcissistic struggle of an oedipal nature by introducing the concept of 'Oedipal configuration'.*[1]

The Oedipal configuration

As we know, the concept of 'Oedipus *complex*' concerns parricide and incest from the point of view of the patient's desire. The concept I have chosen of 'Oedipal *configuration*' constitutes a notion of larger extension than the Oedipus complex. The reason for my proposing this concept springs from the previous works I have just mentioned in which I found myself once and again *linking a certain narcissistic functioning to an oedipal context*. I found the concept of Oedipus complex to be too restrictive to understand the nature of *the patient's identification with a certain narcissistic conflict solution of the parents*. Besides, as we know, the recognition of the differences between the generations and the sexes, as well as of the 'other' as a differentiated person, are essential psychic achievements for the child. But, in his helplessness the child needs the parents to recognize him as differentiated from their own oedipal histories. Of course, this differentiation is only partially fulfilled since the parents always have unconscious desires.

Let us bear in mind that it is by means of a (re)construction in the history of the transference that the patient and the analyst come to have a picture of how the parents' relationship to the patient *might* have been. Freud's concept of the Oedipus complex concerns the unconscious desires of the patient towards the parents and, in my view, it does not encompass the nature and history of the oedipal objects as such. Now, I believe we need a wider concept if we are to study the particular relation among generations that our clinical experience leads us to consider. Let us understand by this relation not only the relation of the child to the parents but also the *parents' relation* to the child as it may be *(re)constructed*. I propose the concept of 'Oedipal configuration' to include this reciprocal relationship between the child and the parents. Nevertheless, we should not forget that it is necessarily a dissymmetric relationship from the very beginning because of the child's helplessness.

According to this standpoint, we can speak of two sides to the patient's Oedipal configuration:

1 On the one hand, the patient's unconscious wishes (death wishes and incestuous desires for both parents); that is, the relation of the child to the parents. This is what we consider as the Oedipus complex.
2 On the other hand, the patient has in his *internal world a certain version of how the parents recognized his 'otherness' and the significance for them of the patient being*

male or female. This version has consequences in the way the patient organizes his oedipal conflicts.[2]

So I consider the 'Oedipus complex' to be a partial aspect of a larger configuration – the tip of the iceberg, as it were.

Alice

When Alice called me for the first time she said: 'Well, I imagine that now I will be obliged to go to your office' as if it were I who had called her. Distance, inaccessibility and silence were destined to become the main characteristics of her analysis. In our first interview, she said that she felt 'elsewhere'; at the same time she was proud that she was an enigma for both parents, whom she described as intrusive and aroused in me the feeling that it might be difficult to get in touch with her, there being a risk in the transference of either leaving her feeling isolated or attacking her with intrusion. So her silence became in her sessions a sort of implicit challenge as if she were saying from the very beginning: 'You will never get to know me.'

At times, Alice could not understand the meaning of my words and even felt at those moments a kind of unspeakable anxiety. These episodes of not understanding and anxiety were unpredictable. She said nothing about them and they remained for weeks as a source of unspoken conflict. Then, a long time after, months or years, she would come back to those episodes claiming that I had said things that were very painful for her, that I had been unjust.

In the session I have chosen for our purpose she begins talking immediately, which is unusual for Alice. She has just begun a new job with which she pays for her analysis. It is a job where she is paid and learns at the same time (what we call in France a *stage*):

> *Alice*: I have to leave this job. It's impossible to go on. The chief just confronts opinions. It is not a situation designed to learn. No hope . . . How would it be possible to learn. They just want to know how the specialists think of the matter. Learning is not a project of this 'programme' [. . .] I don't know what they want of me, as if they wanted me to be a specialist at an international level. [She gives several examples in a vague and tearful way.]

I try to formulate my words as if in a third position, in a decentred listening and a decentred speaking. I want to convey the idea of time, of waiting. This has to do with the feeling of hope. I also hope to find a way of being closer to her private language, to her private discourse, which for the moment, as analyst, I do not have access to (and I imagine she has not either). I also try to put into words two kinds of affect. Her anger, which I can almost feel in my body, and her sadness, which is linked to loss anxiety (mostly detected by me because with this job she pays for her analysis):

> *Analyst*: You seem at the same time sad and furious at not feeling able to be and to do what you imagine is expected of you. For the moment we do not know why you feel that you cannot learn.

I would like to add as a comment for my interpretation that there is an impersonal formulation when I say 'what you imagine is expected of you'. This formulation tends to create an opening of this concrete situation.

> *Alice* [contemptuously]: I never ask questions. My family is like that! This is the way to be: Not to ask questions [. . .]. My father taught me not to ask, but to understand quickly before everybody else [. . .]. The worst thing in the eyes of my whole family is not to be considered intelligent, because then you are necessarily stupid [she uses a French argotic word which means 'silly' and denotes the female genitals: *Con* or *conne*, depending on gender]. [Short silence.] Last year in my other job I did not ask a single question! [She goes on to explain different ways of being intelligent or silly.]

This was the first time she had spoken with such passion and in such detail on the topic of intelligence and the importance of not asking, although she had mentioned an evaluation in which it was said that, 'Alice never asked any questions'. But at the time, it was not clear how proud she was of this evaluation. While I listen to her speaking so contemptuously, I find it difficult to put into words what I am feeling and thinking. I am trying to find words that are close to her private language not yet discovered. I remember at this point that, as a small girl, she was moved abruptly to another country where she could not understand the language. We had reconstructed how difficult it had been for her to understand even what was going on in the kindergarten. But Alice's comment was that the family thought everything was fine because she was very intelligent. The interpretation springs from this spontaneous recollection of mine:

> *Analyst*: Maybe you feel that by asking you become helpless as was the case when you lost your own language. It is hard not to have words even to say you don't understand the words. Maybe you felt better by thinking you were bright and perhaps exceptional while the others were silly, *con*, for not knowing *your* language.

Once again I listened to how she received my interpretation. I am curious to see the effect my words concerning her conflict between helplessness and contempt had on her. She answers immediately with excitement and very engaged: 'At home we are all intelligent . . . except my mother, she is the *conne* of the family!'

I heard the pleasure she expresses when she denigrates her mother and attributes to her all the helplessness I had just interpreted. She goes on, with evident pleasure, to give all sorts of detail and anecdote that demonstrate to her that her mother is manifestly stupid. The analysand's comments are totally unexpected. We have an opening into new material.

This internal mother, as just discovered, is different from the mother of material reality. She is a well-known scholar and writer, much appreciated by French intelligentsia. Then Alice explains how her father will not accept any sign of weakness or helplessness. But she says this very proudly, as though she never needed any affection or protection (as others would need). Through her words I can hear that had she not adopted her father's (phallic) solution she would have nothing, she would be nobody. I also hear how proud she is of following her father and how contemptuous she is of her mother:

> *Alice*: Mother says there's nothing worse than being a woman; she told me she was so disappointed by my being a girl . . . My father taught me to play chess when I was very small, whereas my brothers, who are younger than me, could not even play cards! They too are *con*. [In reality, her brothers are good scientists.] The worst thing I can imagine is to be a victim like my mother! [. . .] Mother told me that father only accepted to marry because he wanted children [. . .]. My grandmother [the mother's mother] always said that my father is both mother and father at the same time; that my mother is a total failure as a mother . . . My grandmother adores my father and always takes his side when my parents quarrel, as they so often do . . . She is always there, deciding [. . .].

The analysand has never before spoken with such a variety of affects. The 'couple' of the grandmother with the father and her contemptuous judgement of her mother are absolutely new material. My attention to how she listens to my interpretations opens up an *unconscious scene* she has never spoken of before. In this scene, there is not only an internal father who knows everything and does not allow ignorance and lack of curiosity, but also the 'mother of the mother' who says 'who has what'. It is the first time I am actually able to hear how her world is divided into those who 'have' and those who 'have not' (and are *con*). I think I am getting closer to her private language and what it means for her to be a woman. When I interpret her psychic pain ('It is hard not to have words even to say you don't understand the words'), her fear of her own helplessness is attributed wholesale to her internal mother ('At home we are all intelligent, except my mother . . . she is the *conne* of the family'). Alice also adds: 'My mother says that nothing is worse than being a woman.' And finally we hear: 'My grandmother says that my mother is a real failure as a mother.' (I did not propose one of the possible interpretations of the transference: 'You feel it is too difficult to learn psychoanalytical language and you want to quit'.)

Now I can hear that she is actually using her private language by the way she associates to my interpretations allowing us to listen to unprecedented material. She is giving us (both her and me) access to a new unconscious scene: Her infantile sexual theory by which she sees women simply as castrated creatures and she does not want to be one. Thus she becomes the double of her father, playing chess in mutual fascination while the younger brothers are castrated (*con*). Who am *I* for her in the transference is an implicit open question.

This was a moment when we partially overcame Alice's psychic inaccessibility, which, as we said, was a constant characteristic of her analysis. Already in this session I could have interpreted how I heard what silence meant for her, but I abstained from doing so, since the opening up of new material, in her own private language, seemed quite enough. We had arrived at listening to an *unconscious link* between what she had said at the beginning of the session ('I have to quit, they want me to be a specialist') *and* 'my grandmother decides who is a complete failure (my mother) and who is complete (my father [who is father–mother])'. I am interested in reconstructing the traces of the earliest significant others. In this case not only father and mother but, as it became evident to me, also *grandmother*.

Now, we could consider the imago of the mother as the consequence of projection and only projection of Alice's aggressivity in the context of oedipal rivalry. The oedipal rivalry is evident. But I believe this point of view can be enriched. I prefer to consider that we are *also* (re)constructing Alice's version of how her mother might have been trying to solve her (the mother's) oedipal conflicts with her own mother, the grandmother. This assumption comes from the analysand's narcissistic way of functioning, which is *associated* with the 'relation-of-the-mother-to-her-own-narcissistic-mother' (Alice's grandmother).

What is the point of adopting this complementary point of view? My aim is to reconstruct how the oedipal objects might have intervened to constitute the patient's psyche – by means of her identifications, precisely, to the object's way of functioning. In this sense, we can consider that there is also transmission of what it means, for her mother, to be a woman. The patient is identified with the unpleasant qualities of what being a woman meant for her mother. From this point of view, sexual differentiation is the result of a 'narcissistic logic' where men are 'complete', therefore valuable, and women are 'incomplete', worthless (*conne*). So, according to this narcissistic phallic logic, the grandmother is 'complete': She decides – in the patient's psyche – who is to have value and who is not. This narcissistic phallic logic is the basis of her infantile sexual theory, already mentioned, whereby she 'sees women simply as castrated creatures and she does not want to be one'.

Alice takes pleasure in saying that the grandmother has chosen the father to be the father–mother; in reducing her mother to being the 'daughter of the

55

grandmother'; in eliminating the mother as a valid sexual partner for the father. In this sense the mother in Alice's *psyche* is immobilized, she cannot change, she is excluded forever. Alice may now analyse this narcissistic assumption, which is linked to the pleasure of telling how her oedipal objects are related to each other . . . through her mother's devaluation. Springing from the narcissistic transference we are in the process of (re)constructing how the oedipal objects are related in Alice's psyche: The grandmother, according to the patient's narrative, is one of those oedipal objects.

Narcissism as a mode of functioning

Let us now reflect on the contradiction that characterizes narcissism. In previous writings I have dealt with the implicit question of whether we can study narcissism in terms of an *intrapsychic conflict*. Considering that this intrapsychic conflict is linked to the history of the constitution of the patient's psyche, my answer is affirmative: It is possible to examine narcissism in terms of an intrapsychic conflict.

In Chapter 1, I expressed the view that:

[T]he narcissistic configuration has a contradictory characteristic: At the same time as expressing his self-sufficiency, the subject needs the other to confirm that he is indeed admirably self-sufficient.

We analysts need a theoretical framework to take account of this contradiction. To this end, I include the notions of intersubjectivity and intrasubjectivity.

My theoretical standpoint, partially developed in previous texts, is different from the current literature on the subject. For the sake of easier communication I choose once again to link the basic assumptions in this essay only with some basic concepts in Freud's metapsychology around 1915. As a crucial difference with current literature *I am not using the concept of narcissism as related to the concept of self*.[3] I shall use the *concept of narcissism exclusively as a particular kind of investment*. I am referring to a *mode of functioning* of the subject in his relation to the world and *not* to a content within the mind. In this perspective, narcissistic cathexis or investment also modifies the object–world. The narcissistic investment is a psychic act that constitutes the 'ego' and contributes to its reorganization.

When I refer to an ego, I am referring to the 'total ego'[4] (*Gesamt-Ich*) and its conflicting relation to the 'pleasure-purified ego', both concepts developed by Freud (1915a, 1921). In my perspective, the constitution of the ego is also ruled by the narcissistic regulation.[5] From a clinical point of view, I have loosely defined a narcissistic relationship by the way the subject *refuses to recognize 'otherness'*, intersubjectivity, because he is functioning according to the narcissistic criteria I have examined.

I shall recall once again Freud's famous passage about 'His Majesty the Baby' – where he says that the parents' love for their children reactivates their own infantile narcissism (Freud 1914b: 91) – to point out that here narcissism is conceived of by Freud as being close to the notion of intersubjectivity I have chosen: From the very beginning the adults are establishing with the child a narcissistic object relation. Freud's point of view can be related to Winnicott's remark (1967) that the baby looks at the way he is seen by his mother. My understanding of narcissism from the standpoint of intersubjectivity[6] is related both to Freud's and Winnicott's metaphors: *I conceive of narcissism always as depending on the other from the very beginning even if the subject cannot recognize the 'other's' intervention as such.*

Recognition of 'otherness' is a momentous step, which marks the passage from the narcissistic mode of functioning to the oedipal modality. Instead of recognizing him for what he actually is and desires (that is for his 'otherness'), the subject who relates through a narcissistic logic sees the 'other' in terms of the degree of pleasure or unpleasure that the 'other' arouses. Even if the subject recognizes the other as such we can also refer to a narcissistic investment when the qualities of the other are considered according to *narcissistic criteria and not according to what the other is and desires.* We can say that there is a potential intrapsychic conflict between the narcissistic functioning and the oedipal level, since at the latter the 'other' should be recognized in his own being and his own desires. Already the concept of 'total ego' (*Gesamt-Ich*) involves a potential conflict with the 'pleasure-purified ego'. In consequence also in this Freudian perspective *narcissism carries in its own organization a potential conflict.*

In my view the *intrinsic conflictual character of narcissism has not been sufficiently underlined or in some cases it has been disregarded altogether.* We must not be led astray by this narcissistic regulation, unpleasure can also rule the intrapsychic conflict of the subject in such a way that he expulses what is felt by him to be valuable and loveable. In this case, the unpleasure comes from keeping both terms of the conflict intrapsychically. Therefore one of the terms of the conflict (which is positively invested) is expelled as a narcissistic conflict solution for unpleasure.

The exorbitant wish that for the child all the necessities and 'the laws of nature and of society' (Freud 1914b: 91) be suspended – even if this could mean a favourable disposition towards the child – appears as an intrusion of the parents' conflicts on him. In this kind of narcissistic object relationship, the child represents the ideal ego of the parents and in some cases he must receive from them not only what the parents had actually received in the past, but also, and specially, what they most lacked. This perspective enables us to understand how the parents can expulse something that is felt to be good as well as the constitution of a negative identity in the child. Narcissistic regulation is also an essential component in the pleasure that the individual takes in loving and in thinking. This essential aspect related to self-esteem is not considered here.

One question seems in order: *Whose* narcissism are we talking about, that of the patient or that of the parents? In psychoanalysis, in the setting of the session, we can only speak of the patient's narcissism. However, because the patient is partially identified with the narcissistic logic with which the parents functioned we can (re)construct, first, a kind of internal parent representation and, second, how the parents' narcissism *might* actually have been directed towards him. In other words, the patient identifies with the parents' intrapsychic struggle, with their mode of conflict solution.[7,8]

If we bear in mind that narcissistic object regulation is, according to my hypothesis, *one* of the ways in which all patients function psychically, we can say that the narcissistic modality might be reactivated in each and *every* analysis, as my clinical experience leads me to think. Here we can measure the interest in adopting as a theoretical frame in which to work the concept of Oedipal configuration and its narcissistic dimension.

Narcissistic transference

Considering that narcissism prevented the establishment of a transference, Freud believed that narcissism set a limit to analysis. Of course, many analysts after Freud, working along the path opened by 'Mourning and melancholia' (Freud, 1917a [1915]) have recognized narcissistic transference. This underlines the importance of the theoretical context in which each analyst can best listen to and analyse the narcissistic way of functioning of the patient.

I consider narcissistic transference on the basis of the contradictory configuration of narcissism and by resorting to the concepts of intersubjectivity and intrasubjectivity. In the narcissistic transference, the patient might need the analyst just to *confirm that he does not need him*. So he would not be able to experience his narcissistic achievement without the other. The struggle against the narcissistic parent, which in my view is a momentous step in the analysis of the oedipal conflict, is re-enacted in the transference.

Coming back for a moment to the case of Alice, we are able to explain some of the meanings silence has for her. In this kind of transference of a narcissistic nature I am supposed not to need her words, I am self-sufficient and keep everything for myself. Yet, in another level, I am 'silly' and I do not know . . . unless I ask. At the same time she never misses her sessions, even if she often remains silent, because she needs *me* to confirm that she does not need me as an analyst: Her fragility and omnipotence express in the transference, precisely, the contradictory structure by which I have characterized narcissism.

Parricide and the Oedipal configuration

Let us begin by considering how Freud dealt with parricide, since this is one of the key concepts of the Oedipus complex. In 1900 Freud, keen on asserting the universality of the Oedipus complex, was not primarily interested in looking for any cause of parricide and incest. The Oedipus complex is organized around the way the subject deals with his unconscious parricidal and incestuous desires for both parents.

Staying with Freud, we may consider parricide from a different point of view. In *Totem and Taboo* (Freud 1912–13) the problem of parricide is seen as a *response* to a crucial issue: How can young males negotiate their sexuality in the face of the mythical figure embodied by the Primitive Father who has the absolute and exclusive right to possess all women? I consider this father figure as a narcissistic father, the only one to have absolute power. Thus parricide and incest can be understood also, but not only, from the point of view of a narcissistic struggle. This fight is based on the narcissistic illusion that there is only *one psychic space* where there is forever a unique erotic object. And this unique space belongs entirely to the narcissistic father; he is narcissistic, precisely because he has power to rule in this unique space and to decide *who is to have what*. The father becomes a father of an oedipal nature when he forbids *one* specific woman and allows his son to have an *exogamic project* for his future.[9]

I propose to use the narcissistic father of *Totem and Taboo* as a metaphor of the narcissistic nature of certain figures of the father. By conceiving of an Oedipal configuration that covers a wider range of oedipal conflicts and by conceiving of a narcissistic dimension of the Oedipal configuration, I propose a conceptual matrix to link the patient's narcissistic way of functioning to his 'Oedipus complex'.

While considering the status of the narcissistic parent, I am trying to avoid the consequences of a *solipsistic* theory, based *exclusively* on projection. It should not be taken for granted that the narcissistic parent is *always and only* the consequence of a projection of the parricidal wishes of the child. This allows us, along with the patient, to make an analysis not only of the parents' imago but also of a partially reconstructed picture of how the original objects might have *intervened* for or against what might loosely be called an oedipal relinquishing. This is always a hypothetical construction. Thus, we can (re)construct in the history of the transference a narcissistic parent that does not allow the child to have his own psychic space. And once again, why should we regard as anecdotal those fragments of the patient's history that are so intimately linked to the parents' history as reconstructed?

'Who was I for my parents? What did they want of me?' These questions that crop up very often in the course of an analysis point to a (re)construction of how the parents might have been. When the answer is that they wanted everything; when the answer is that they wanted what *they* needed me to be, then the discovery of these basic unconscious parental assumptions by which the patient's narcissism has been regulated allows a new and crucial implicit question to be formulated in the transference: 'In this repetitive but still new way of being "me", am I allowed to hope that you, the analyst, accept me in terms that are different from those I believed were my parents' unconscious basic assumptions?' Here, transference can also be transformation.

My aim is not to raise the question of whether all men wish to kill their father and marry their mother (the positive Oedipus complex), but rather to consider, in the face of this universal and indestructible desire, what the particular relation is between generations, what the conditions are that make it possible to work through the oedipal paradox: 'You shall resemble your father in some ways and at the same time you shall not!' The concept of Oedipal configuration includes, precisely, this filial constellation, the relation between generations.

Moreover in the patient's psyche the oedipal objects relate to each other according to the narcissistic criteria we have just mentioned: The grandmother constitutes a narcissistic parent. Here, again, we see what impelled me to reflect on narcissism in terms of a narcissistic investment, a mode of psychic functioning.

The grandparent as a narcissistic parent

Being the grandmother (in the case of Alice), of one of the oedipal objects and having the qualities of a narcissistic parent, I consider it legitimate to call this particular mode of psychic functioning of the analysand the 'narcissistic dimension of the Oedipal configuration'.

Let us consider in some detail this narcissistic dimension of the Oedipal configuration. In Alice's psyche, the mother appears as the daughter of a narcissistic mother, the grandmother. Alice and her mother appear in the patient's mind as if they were *sisters before* the *only possible mother*, a narcissistic mother, the grandmother. The difference between generations has been blurred: There is a 'telescoping of generations'. All this leads me to think that *Alice has been using this history unconsciously to resist – for narcissistic purposes – any recognition of the parents' sexuality as a couple*. In other words, the *narcissistic resistance* she opposes in recognizing the oedipal conflicts, the 'Oedipus complex', *has a history* that is interwoven with the parent's history (as reconstructed).

I am not speaking of the mother or of the grandmother; neither am I referring to of any original object from the standpoint of material reality. I am talking of the way in which they appear as part of an unconscious intrapsychic conflict in the *patient's* psyche. To better enlighten this purpose, let us see how these objects change with the working through of the narcissistic dimension. In a session that occurred one year and five months later, after a silence that lasted nearly the entire session:

Alice: I am absolutely astonished because I saw Marcia practising her music lesson very slowly and I realized that I must have learnt music in the same way. I cannot remember how it was; I cannot imagine me not-knowing. I have forgotten every single moment of my learning. As if I had always known . . . [Thoughtful silence.] This makes me think about my state of hopelessness when, in my job, I feel I don't know. It is as if I could never learn, as if I had to know everything immediately, time does not pass. [Short silence.] You know . . . I think my parents wanted us, my brothers and me, to do things perfectly . . . but I don't believe they were so critical as I always said they were . . . in fact they encouraged us to learn . . . For instance, when we left the country and I had to learn the language, my parents encouraged us very much. I remember they came and said: You are our 'Petit Larousse Illustré' . . . and that was a game by which they meant we had learned quite a lot. They were very supportive . . . [Silence.] You cannot imagine how deeply shocked I was seeing Marcia studying. It was a slap in my face! This brought me to reality. So I had also learned, as she was learning! For example, to type on the machine. I always thought I had known how to do it from the beginning and that I always typed the papers for my parents without having to learn. I learnt to play the piano when I was only six . . . I realize, only now can I say that I began to learn music at that age. I used to say, I have played the piano since I was six. [She gives many other examples, her playing chess, her learning different subjects.]

She remains silent and then she addresses to me in a direct way:

Alice: I am afraid you might not realize how important what I have just discovered is.
Analyst: Have I learnt it in analysis?
Alice: You know, I have been always elsewhere . . . As if time had stopped for ever . . . If I begin to learn and to commit myself in my analysis and in my job, then I feel time is really passing, and I am so afraid!
Analyst: Afraid and wondering if I would accept you as you feel you are, not having, not knowing, asking questions, taking your time, learning . . . [Alice is listening to my words and remains in thoughtful silence.]

This is the end of the session.

Here, above all, the parents are a couple who grant equal rights to the three children: The phallic logic we have mentioned is not ruling in this session. *There is no more blurring of generations.* The parents in Alice's intrapsychic reality are playing with them; and with humour (the protective aspects of the superego, Freud 1927b: 165–6) they can anticipate with the children what they can get to know in the future (the dictionary), recognizing what they have already learned.

Alice partially overcomes the narcissistic struggle (she came to experience not-knowing as a narcissistic blow, 'a slap in the face') and the oedipal couple begins to be recognized in her psychic reality. What the patient calls her 'not-knowing' *is now related to the oedipal exclusion – the 'Oedipus complex' – and no more to a hopeless narcissistic issue.* Past is constructed as such. Now, in the transference, Alice is somewhere and has a potential project for the future.

To sum up what has been said, let us recall that from my viewpoint the narcissistic struggle against the oedipal objects is *inevitable.* By taking into account the narcissistic dimension of the Oedipal configuration we can help patients to have a better access to their psychic truths and to work through a psychic space of their own.

6

THE OEDIPUS MYTH
REVISITED (1993)*

Introduction

The idea of revisiting the Oedipus myth came to me when I was reflecting on the theoretical problems that sprang from my clinical experience. Some ideas cropped up again and again, which made me think it would be worthwhile. Could this myth help solve some theoretical problems I had been working on in the previous essay? I hope to convey my key ideas in the course of this essay.

First, I had encountered a seminal problem in my psychoanalytical experience. We have, with the patient, to work through *both his narcissistic omnipotent illusions and his responsibility for his unconscious oedipal desires.* In his narcissistic beliefs man may have the chimeric illusion that he can completely govern his destiny. Thus, on the one hand, the subject has a narcissistic illusion of being 'the master in his own house' (Freud 1917b), while, on the other hand, he is irredeemably 'elsewhere' because of his unconscious identifications and unconscious desires. Yet psychoanalysis teaches us (and unconscious guilt is an example) how responsible we are for our psychic truths, for our unconscious desires, which are always active. Furthermore, I was struck by the status of what remains secret in the transmission of certain unconscious identifications.

In this essay I am taking material we can all share, the Oedipus myth, as another way of conveying how my clinical experience has led me to think in terms of the concept of an Oedipal *configuration*. The main questions that interested me were why did Oedipus commit parricide and incest in material reality? Where does Oedipus' psychic responsibility for his destiny lie? What is Laius' status in the tragedy?

---

* First presented at a 'meet an author' annual colloquium, 'Groupe de Lyon' of the Paris Psychoanalytical Society on 19 June 1993.

My question is whether the Oedipus complex[1] concept is sufficient to help us to understand why Oedipus committed parricide (and incest). Perhaps we shall see again how I came up with the concept of 'Oedipal configuration'.

From a methodological standpoint the aim of this essay is to use the myth as it is recounted by Robert Graves (Graves 1955, Vol. 2: 9–10) and not in Sophocles' tragedies or any other version of the myth. I am only using part of the myth and the version I have chosen is a very simple one. Ironically, the author of this version, a mythologist, happened to be very strongly opposed to any psychoanalytical interpretation of this myth (or any myth). Sophocles' *Oedipus Rex* and *Oedipus in Colonus* are wonderful narratives. But the simple version I have chosen is adequate for the issues I want to explore that are both fundamental and circumscribed at the same time. I am using the myth as a metaphor to explore certain psychoanalytical issues and not to analyse the myth as such.

I shall focus on the problem of *filicide–parricide* in particular. The incest is considered only as part of the prophecy, but my analysis in fact stops with Laius' death. Therefore *Jocasta is only seen from Laius' point of view*; I do not take into account Oedipus' investigation of his own past, which is a fundamental subject; so Tiresias is absent as well as Oedipus' and Jocasta's children; even the unavoidable riddle of the Sphinx is not taken into account. These aspects of the myth would deserve another essay in themselves and do not come into the scope of this essay. Nevertheless, I have taken into account Didier Anzieu's methodological recommendation that the text of the myth be considered as a whole (Anzieu 1970). I think there is no essential contradiction between placing stress on these aspects of the myth to make my point and the way I understand the myth in its entirety.

The Oedipus myth

To begin with I want to give a brief sketch of some general ideas that will then be considered from a strictly psychoanalytical point of view. The Oedipus myth tells us that parricide and incest are abominable. I believe that all the variants of the myth set out from this basic assumption.

Because parricide and incest *are* abominable, human destiny (in our culture?) consists in ensuring that they do not take place in material reality. Oedipus remains a tragic figure, not because he does not share the essential values of human *Dasein* – revulsion of parricide and incest. On the contrary, he shares them and in an extremely explicit way. I want, in particular, to revisit at this point one aspect of the myth that, in my view, is generally neglected. Oedipus' inability to prevent himself from acting in a way regarded by everyone, including himself, as abominable – which makes it a tragedy – stems from the fact that *Oedipus' destiny is ruled by deceit.*

I want to put forward my first hypothesis that Oedipus' destiny is *not* governed solely *by the prophecy* – by a message that we might describe as 'positive' – but that the prophecy is linked to an *unspoken message* – a message that we might describe as 'negative'.

Secrecy relates to both adoption and the original filicide. So I propose to examine this 'negative message' concerning the secret of Oedipus' origins. In my analysis, I shall try to grasp the essence of this unspoken message and to see its effects (if any) on Oedipus' destiny. I have not encountered any psycho-analytical interpretation of the Oedipus myth that gives a *predominant* status to the secret character of Oedipus' genealogy. Filicide has also been largely neglected by psychoanalysts,[2,3] starting with Freud himself.[4] Let us now look at some features of the Oedipus myth selected from the narrative by Robert Graves:

Laius, son of Labdacus, married Jocasta, and ruled over Thebes. Grieved by his prolonged childlessness, he *secretly* consulted the Delphic Oracle, which informed him that this seeming misfortune was a blessing, because *any child born to Jocasta would become his murderer. He therefore put Jocasta away, though without offering any reason for his decision,* which caused her such vexation that, *having made* him drunk, she inveigled him into her arms again as soon as night fell. When, nine months later, Jocasta was brought to bed of a son, Laius snatched him from the nurse's arms, pierced his feet with a nail and, binding them together, exposed him on Mount Cithaeron.

Yet the Fates had ruled that this boy should reach a ripe old age. A Corinthian shepherd found him, *named him Oedipus because his feet were deformed by the nail-wound,* and brought him to Corinth, where King Polybus was reigning at the time.

According to another version of the story, Laius did not expose Oedipus on the mountain, but locked him in a chest, which was lowered into the sea from a ship. This chest drifted ashore at Sicyon, where Periboea, Polybus' queen, happened to be on the beach, supervising her royal laundry-women. She picked up Oedipus, retired to a thicket and *pretended* to have been overcome by the pangs of labour. Since the laundry-women were too busy to notice what she was about she *deceived* them all into thinking that he had only just been born. But Periboea *told the truth* to Polybus who, also being childless, was pleased to rear Oedipus as his own son.

One day, *taunted by a Corinthian youth with not in the least resembling his supposed parents, Oedipus went to ask the Delphic Oracle what future lay in store for him. 'Away from the shrine, wretch!' the Pythoness cried in disgust. 'You will kill your father and marry your mother!'*

Since Oedipus loved Polybus and Periboea, and shrank from bringing disaster upon them, he at once decided against returning to Corinth. But in the *narrow* defile between Delphi and Daulis he happened to meet Laius, who ordered him roughly to step off the road and *make way for his betters;* Laius, it should be explained, was in a chariot and Oedipus on foot. Oedipus retorted that he acknowledged no betters except the gods and *his own parents*.

'So much the worse for you!' cried Laius, and ordered his charioteer Polyphontes to drive on.

One of the wheels *bruised Oedipus' foot* and, transported by rage, he killed Polyphontes with his spear. Then, flinging Laius on the road entangled in the reins, and whipping up the team, he made them drag him to death. It was left to the king of Plataeae to bury both corpses.

Laius had been on his way to ask the Oracle how he might rid Thebes of the Sphinx.

(Graves 1955: 9–10 (emphasis added))

Forms of deceit in the Oedipus myth

Now let us return to my conjecture that because Oedipus' destiny is ruled by deceit he cannot avoid committing in material reality what he considers to be abominable (parricide and incest). This leads us briefly to reconsider some forms of deceit in the Oedipus myth that are relevant here, before moving on to a psychoanalytical exploration. Throughout this narrative of the myth we find that deceit is at the *base* of Oedipus' conception.

When Laius consults the oracle he is warned that any son he might have with Jocasta would necessarily commit parricide. In Graves' version, incest is only mentioned when Oedipus consults the oracle himself later on. So, according to the prophecy, Jocasta could *only give him a parricide as a son*. The only way that Laius finds to avoid that fate happens to be deception. So we cannot neglect the significance that Jocasta has for Laius. Here the standpoint I have chosen considers only Laius' desires and his mistrust of Jocasta. In some versions of the myth it is said that Laius' sterility is a punishment for his homosexuality. Jocasta, in her turn, cheats to circumvent the unexplained narcissistic wound inflicted by her husband. In the myth Oedipus does not know the parental status Laius and Jocasta hold for him, and that Laius did not want him to be conceived or wanted him to be killed. Oedipus ignores both the meaning of his name, which derives from the attempted filicide, and the fact that Polybus and Periboea adopted him in secret. Oedipus' consultation of the oracle leads him to listen to the prophecy that, unbeknown to him, governs his destiny. Finally when Oedipus seeks to flee this parricidal and incestuous destiny, he, in fact, becomes entangled in it, insofar as he *does not know that he does not know* who his parents are.

Oedipus' 'Oedipus complex'

We usually acknowledge after Freud, from a psychoanalytical perspective, that the Oedipus myth concerns Oedipus' parricidal and incestuous desires and we view them as a paradigm of the unconscious desires felt by all men for their parents. This paradigm is usually called the 'direct Oedipus complex'. Let us repeat it once again, Oedipus' destiny is not governed solely by the prophecy – by what, according to what just has been said, can legitimately be called the 'Oedipus *complex*' – but also by an unspoken message. For Oedipus the secrets surrounding both his adoption and the original filicide are radical and cause him to lose his bearings as to his genealogy. In this sense, he is also radically ignorant of the identity of what we shall call, not without irony, his 'oedipal' objects that, as we know, Oedipus wishes to protect. In the myth, the prohibition to commit parricide and incest cannot be linked to what can be called recognizable, symbolic oedipal objects but only to unknown (biological) parental objects.[5]

Considered from this angle, when Oedipus gets in touch with his unconscious desires (by means of the prophecy), i.e. his 'Oedipus complex', the secret concerning his parentage becomes the logical *cause* of the inescapability of Oedipus' destiny. It is not enough to say that Oedipus, like all human beings, has a psychic responsibility, as he certainly has, for his 'Oedipus complex'. We must also ask a theoretical question as to what *the conditions* are that would enable Oedipus and any human being to relinquish acting out the 'Oedipus complex' in actual material reality. In other words, what is the *particular relation between generations* that makes it possible to work through the paradox of the 'Oedipus complex': 'You shall resemble your father (in some ways) and at the same time you shall not (in other ways)!' This is a key question we shall explore.

Because Oedipus' (supposed) parents have adopted him in secret, the father (and the mother) to whom the oracle refers are unknown. But from the standpoint of the logic that rules the myth, the prohibition against parricide and incest (a prohibition accepted by everyone) concerns only Laius as the father and only Jocasta as the mother. Consequently, Oedipus is subjected to a law in which he believes profoundly but that, by definition, he cannot observe insofar as he does not possess bearings for its fulfillment. Oedipus does not know that he is ignorant of his genealogy. *The myth is ruled by a logic that is a paradox in itself.* Whatever Oedipus decides, he cannot accomplish the commandments of the law. Let me suggest a second complementary hypothesis: *The filial system*, the relation of parentage to which somebody is related *is a necessary condition* to identify the 'oedipal objects' and in this sense it guarantees a protective function.

If we were to sum up both hypotheses, we could say that Oedipus' filial system is blurred by deceit and therefore he has no way of finding his bearings, in relinquishing parricide and incest. On the one hand, Oedipus' ignorance of his origins and the origin of his name that is linked to filicide and, on the other hand, the secrecy in which his adoption is kept, represent key features of the tragedy.

The unspoken question

I find myself proposing a rather radical change of perspective in regard to those characteristics on which we usually focus as psychoanalysts when considering the myth. Let us analyse step by step what could be the *effects* in the enactment of Oedipus' destiny of the fact that his filial system is blurred by deceit.

First, the secret concerning Oedipus' parentage weighs on him throughout his life, one of the reasons being that human sexuality is organized at two different points in time. Thus (would it be on the threshold of adolescence?), Oedipus consults the oracle himself. The oracle knocks twice: Once for Laius and once for Oedipus.

Second, in the myth, as recounted by Graves, Oedipus consults the oracle because he has been taunted that he does not resemble his parents. In this question, he is asking the oracle not for an explicit answer as concerns his genealogy, as we might expect, but one concerning his destiny. There is a hidden aspect to this consultation if we take into account his concern about not resembling his parents. Oedipus is unconsciously asking for his *origins*, for something that has already happened. *He takes as a problem of the future what in fact is a problem of the past.* Thus this question has an *enigma* in itself, an unknown aspect for the person who is asking.[6] Oedipus is unconsciously asking: *Why* '[do I] not in the least resemble my [supposed] parents?' 'He does not know that he does not know' is a formulation I have proposed on several occasions that here raises a question. It seems as if Oedipus knew what it was that he 'should not ask'.[7]

Third (if we bear in mind this question about his genealogy), although Oedipus puts the question in terms of 'what future lies in store for me' we might say that unconsciously he is essentially asking: '*Who am I*, where do I come from?' Thus, we could understand the oracle's reply as being: *'You are "He" who will kill his father and marry his mother.'*[8]

In the explicit dialogue nothing is said about the real secret, about what lies at the roots of the consultation itself (not resembling his parents, i.e. his genealogy). This silenced conflict between 'who are the parents' in the question *and* in the answer is essential for the understanding of Oedipus' destiny. By 'who' I mean both that Laius is the '*unknown*' *father* and that he is this kind of father, *a filicidal father.* (The question 'who' Jocasta is deserves a study in itself.)

The Oedipus myth as a
metaphor of a metapsychological concept

Let us bear in mind that my aim is to use, from a methodological standpoint, the myth as a metaphor to explore psychoanalytic problems and not to analyse the myth as such. This comment is a response to Graves' opinion (shared with others) that a myth should only be interpreted in the context of the myth. If we consider, as we are doing, not merely a partial aspect of the Oedipus myth but the myth in its entirety, we cannot fail to see that the act of parricide actually perpetrated by Oedipus is the culmination of a complex process.

The first idea to suggest itself – which to my mind we cannot dismiss out of hand – is that Laius decided on Oedipus' death even before he was born. Laius' *interpretation* – that a son *means only a parricidal son* – is at the root of Oedipus' preordained destiny. The meaning that Laius attaches to Oedipus' existence and the *murderous acting out of this meaning (filicide)* are essential issues. So, *the meaning for Laius of Oedipus being a male and how he refuses Oedipus' otherness, becomes a key condition* for the way Oedipus acts out his 'Oedipus complex'.

The fruit of my reflection on this subject is that it is *not only a question of Oedipus' 'Oedipus complex'* (so to speak) but also *a question of who the 'oedipal' objects are*, how these oedipal objects accepted Oedipus' otherness and the meaning for them of Oedipus being a male. At this point in the analysis of the myth, we find once again the reasons, based on my clinical experience, that led me to think up the concept of 'Oedipal configuration'. By thus assuming a more complex 'Oedipal configuration', I try to avoid reducing the theoretical analysis (as complex and subtle as it may be) to no more than the interplay of drives (without underestimating either the theoretical importance of drives) and to set them within a more complex configuration.

The concept of the Oedipal configuration permits us to ask the crucial question we are exploring in this paper, related to Oedipus' 'neurosis of Destiny' (so to speak): What is the Oedipal configuration that makes it possible to work through the Oedipal conflicts, including the 'Oedipus complex' and also prevents their being acted out in material reality?

If I spoke (from a metapsychological point of view) only of the concept of the 'Oedipus complex' *I could not give a theoretical status* either to the radical secret concerning Oedipus' filial system; to the influence that Laius exerts on Oedipus' destiny by being an unknown filicidal father; or to some of Oedipus' 'oedipal conflicts', for example the fact that Oedipus also accomplishes in reality *what Laius feared most* (and not only what he, Oedipus, feared). To my mind, the importance of this broader approach to oedipal conflicts is that it makes it possible to *link dialectically and on a metapsychological basis the problems of narcissism with oedipal-related issues.*

Oedipus' unconscious concern when consulting the oracle is also a narcissistic concern. He is asking 'Who am I?' and 'Where do I come from?' At the same time this question is dialectically linked to his 'Oedipus complex'. By means of the concept of the Oedipal configuration we avoid the risk of studying narcissism isolated from the oedipal dimension. Finally, as we shall see, without the concept of the Oedipal configuration I could not give a theoretical status to a 'narcissistic father' (Laius) and differentiate him from an oedipal father.

Laius as a metaphor of a metapsychological concept

Some theoretical reflections

I hope it is clear at this point that my aim is not to raise the question of whether all men have unconscious murderous wishes and unconscious incestuous desires for both parents (the 'Oedipus complex'), but to consider in the face of this essential, universal and indestructible desire: (a) Which is the Oedipal config-uration that makes it possible to work through the oedipal conflicts (including the 'Oedipus complex')? (b) What are the conditions that allow Oedipus to actually accomplish in material reality what Laius fears the most as regards his son (i.e. the oracle's prophecy)? (c) What sort of object is Laius for Oedipus' destiny?

I would begin by pointing out that filicide appears to be an excessive response to what a male child *means* for Laius. In this tyrannical way of deciding on the life and death of his son, Laius may be seen as a paradigm of the narcissistic father.[9] Why am I so interested in raising the question of the status of the narcissistic father? My aim is to avoid as much as possible the consequences of a theory based *exclusively* on projection that gives a *solipsistic* solution to the psychoanalytical status of certain narcissistic parents. We could consider Laius as an imago, a consequence of the projection and only of the projection of Oedipus' aggressiveness in the context of oedipal rivalry. This is 'the direct Oedipus complex'.

If we take into account, as I believe we have to, certain characteristics of Laius, we come to grasp one of the reasons that drove me to conceive of an Oedipal configuration. By giving a status to the narcissistic filicidal parent we try to get out of a solipsistic model and find a dialectical matrix for the different dimensions of the *Oedipal* issues we have been studying in the Oedipus myth, including the 'Oedipus complex'.

Although in analysis each and every patient is responsible for his unconscious desires and for his psychic activity, including his 'Oedipus complex', it is essential also to:

1 Recognize the patient's unconscious identification with a 'narcissistic-father'.
2 Be able to recognize the patient's pain of not having been loved.
3 Sometimes even get in touch with the patient's unthinkable anxiety of not

having been desired as a living child: The relation to a Laius–father. I am here talking of the psychoanalytical status of the filicidal parent (father or mother).

Laius as a filicidal narcissistic father

According to Graves, Laius *provokes* Oedipus by ordering him roughly 'to step off the road and make way for his betters'. Oedipus retorts that he acknowledges no betters 'except the gods and his own *parents*' [emphasis added]. We must remember as well that on two occasions in the myth, at two different moments in Oedipus' life, Laius tries to kill his son.[10] The second time, meeting someone who, from the point of view of his generation, *could* be his son, he provokes him. But this time, Oedipus is no longer the helpless infant he once was. In fact, the parricidal logic feared *both* by Laius and by Oedipus predominates and Oedipus' uncertainty about his *genealogy* is decisive for the fulfillment of the prophecy. Oedipus' foot is wounded for the second time. We can see this either as a metaphor for the reactivation of bodily 'memories' of how the attempted filicide occurred or, as I prefer, as a metaphor for the reactivation by the psychical injury of the unthinkable agony of secret filicide linked to his name, Oedipus.

Thus, the *mise en scène* of the myth shows the reactivation for Oedipus of a very complex drama: Rivalry with a man who from the point of view of his generation *could* be his father (he was in touch with his 'oedipal' desires just coming from the oracle) and a secret history of filicide and adoption. In the myth we have a *mise en scène* of a *narcissistic space*: 'In the *narrow defile* [. . .] he happened to meet Laius.' There is only *one* possible psychic space and a *narcissistic* rivalry is expressed in terms of death. *The death of Laius springs from this situation.* As a consequence of this narcissistic way of functioning there is a single narcissistic object of pleasure (Jocasta): Two differentiated objects of pleasure for two different subjects cannot be imagined. The son is regarded as a narcissistic double and *no psychic time or space is left for him*.

We have, then, a paradoxical status for these objects. Jocasta and Laius being the paradigmatic parents of the Oedipus myth and of the 'Oedipus complex', in the way Laius sees Jocasta, they are characterized each of them and both of them together as the only possible erotic couple for ever. In this sense, paradoxical as it may seem, *this oedipal couple has also a narcissistic characteristic.* Here I am exploring *oedipal conflicts of a narcissistic nature* and this paradox can be understood as a 'narcissistic dimension of the Oedipal configuration'.

The myth at this stage says nothing about Jocasta. Could we understand this omission as a lack of intervention on Jocasta's part? In what way could she have intervened? First and foremost, she could have conveyed to Laius that Oedipus would not represent everything for her. Let us recall that in order to prevent the prophecy from being fulfilled Laius ceases to have relations with his wife; and there exists also the reference to his homosexuality. In this context the erotic status of Jocasta appears very dubious. This could explain why Laius is not confident that Jocasta will be a good messenger for conveying to the son the existence of an erotic relationship between the parents. From this perspective, Jocasta fails to transmit the message concerning both the father's threat of castration and the protective barrier against incest. We can see Jocasta as having a negative function in the myth. She does not refute what Laius feared most.

Another myth, this one created by Freud, could give us another metaphor to speak of the status of the narcissistic father. Didier Anzieu (1970: 114) says that in *Totem and Taboo*, Freud invents a myth, the myth of the primitive horde, the killing of the father and the totemic meal, a myth that expresses the foundation of a new moral and social organization. Therefore in *Totem and Taboo*, Freud looks for the *cause of parricide*, and finds it in the necessity of killing what I am willing to call the narcissistic father. Laius and the primitive father are metaphors for the narcissistic father.

Further theoretical reflections

Still from the psychoanalytical perspective I have chosen (and not from a mythologist's point of view about the function of oracles in myths), the answer the oracle gives to Laius can legitimately be seen as an interpretation of what any son means to Laius. Furthermore *this interpretation*, the parricidal son, *leads to Laius' criminal enactment*. We could say that Laius sees himself as killing out of self-defence. Considered from this perspective, Laius is the *filicide of a parricide*. On the one hand, parricide is (as a universal unconscious desire, the conception of the 'Oedipus complex') a first logical and chronological step. On the other hand, filicide, enacted by Laius in material reality, appears in my analysis as the first logical and chronological step towards understanding Oedipus' destiny.

However, when I say that 'Laius sees Oedipus as the parricidal (and incestuous) son, that all male offspring are in his psychic reality' we come up against a serious theoretical problem. *What can we do to guard against an endless transmission* by taking into account a chain of desires for which no solution seems to exist? How many generations would it take to put an end to this kind of transmission of parricide and incest?

My aim is *not* to trace back the Oedipus complex *ad infinitum*, which would amount to no more than *reformulating the same theoretical problems that arise from the concept of the Oedipus complex at another point in time*.[11] To make the point in this metapsychological level we could ask (not without irony) whose Oedipus complex (so to speak!) are we considering, Laius' or Oedipus'? My purpose has been to discover what kind of function Laius has in the Oedipus myth and how this function could be articulated with *Oedipus'* Oedipus complex.

At one stage I felt tempted to speak of a 'Laius complex'.[12] But I realized that my concern was not so much a question of defining two different complexes as one of understanding the following problems: What is the difference between what I call an *oedipal logic* and a *narcissistic logic*? What is the difference between an oedipal father and a narcissistic father?[13]

Laius, as the paradigm of the narcissistic father, is shown in the myth as considering that there is a *unique psychic space* (as a consequence of his narcissistic object regulation) with a *unique erotic object* of love and hate *forever*. This space is dominated, precisely, by the narcissistic father. This method of functioning gives *a narcissistic solution to oedipal rivalry* (or perhaps we should call it hate?): One must live and the other must die; a 'filicide–parricide' logic.

When Laius provokes him, Oedipus cannot flee his preordained destiny. The narcissistic logic prevails. In the myth, the dominance of this narcissistic logic is *perpetuated by deception* insofar as Oedipus' filial system is blurred, precisely, by deceit. Oedipus does not recognize Laius as 'the' oedipal object and he acts out *Laius' fear of having a parricidal son in addition to his own fear.*

An objection could be raised in relation to the psychoanalytical status I give to deceit:[14] Unconscious desires are, by definition, unknown to the subject and an individual feels betrayed by this unconscious dimension. This is true. We are not the owners of our minds. And this narcissistic wound is to be taken into account. Nevertheless, by deceit I am referring not only to the unconscious dimension that Freud discovered. Freud gives a status to these unconscious universal desires by inventing the concept of 'Oedipus complex'. From a psychoanalytical perspective the oracle's prophecy can be understood as one of the possible narratives of this 'complex'. By deceit I am pointing not to what could be conceptualized as repression from a metapsychological standpoint, but to a different mechanism, disavowal maybe (*Verleugnung* [Freud 1927a]).[15]

Unlike Laius (or the father of the primitive horde) as a narcissistic father, a father functions as an oedipal father when he forbids *one* specific woman and can imagine an *exogamic project* for the future of his son. The filial system has a protective function against the acting out of parricide and incest. All the protagonists of the Oedipus triangle are submitted to what I propose to call the oedipal law: *Nobody in the oedipal triangle (which is a dissymmetric triangle) has everything. Nobody is everything for one of the other protagonists of the triangle. Unlike the narcissistic law, nobody has the absolute power to rule another's destiny.*

Now, for the sake of a better understanding, let us remember one of the aims of this essay according to which I have also been using the myth as a metaphor to think up a contradictory and complex issue that all patients have to overcome: That is, the coexistence of both omnipotent illusions of a narcissistic nature and psychic responsibility for the unconscious (oedipal) desires. And in relation to this problem, *I do not want to fall into the trap of inverting the situation of parricide and focusing exclusively on filicide imagining that in the myth Oedipus is absolutely 'innocent'.* From the analytical standpoint adopted, Oedipus is psychically responsible for his unconscious desires. Furthermore, unconscious desires, whether parricidal, incestuous or whatever, are always active. But is Oedipus fully responsible for the acting out of his unconscious desires?[16] In other words, what is then the relationship between, on the one hand, Oedipus' psychic responsibility for his own psychic truths (and the working through of what we could also call in his case an 'oedipal' relinquishing) and, on the other, a struggle with an unknown filicidal father?

In the myth, *Oedipus' responsibility for his unconscious desires is alienated by a narcissistic logic that is perpetuated by filicide and deceit.* We could perhaps say, in addition, that Oedipus does not ask the oracle 'where he comes from', 'who he is', as a way of avoiding the acknowledgement that his whole life has been based on deceit.

If, just for one moment, we take Oedipus as a metaphor for a patient, we could imagine him in the process of reconstructing his history and getting in touch with different levels of psychic truths: (a) His responsibility for his unconscious desires, parricide and incest; (b) putting himself through the unthinkable anxiety of imagining that he could have not existed at all. Here, filicide and secret adoption can be related to a certain version of 'the primal scene' (in this case, the scene of our conception).

I hope that now it is clear why I think that the concept of the Oedipal configuration permits us to give a theoretical status to this particular relation between generations and to the status of the patient's parents. Here, the model of the myth offers us its own limits because in the psychoanalytical process nothing can be said about what characteristics the analysand's parents had in material reality. Nevertheless we cannot dismiss what this myth leads us to think in relation to psychic truths. In these issues the history of the transference gives us a hint. We (re)construct in the history of the transference how the patient's parents *might* have been. *(Re)construction is a key concept to partially overcome these solipsistic issues.*

Final remarks

To our key question of what the particular relation is between generations that makes it possible to work through the paradox of the Oedipus complex, some possible answers could be proposed:

- According to the destructive consequences of deceit in Oedipus' destiny, one conclusion could be that secrets about parentage could destroy the patient's *trust* in psychic truths.
- According to the murderous consequences of Laius' narcissistic version of what a son meant for him, another conclusion could be that collusion, between, on the one hand, the child's *inevitable* narcissistic struggle in the working through of his oedipal conflicts and, on the other, the narcissistic parents' filicidal tendencies, would confirm the patient's illusion of a unique

psychic space and could lead to the destruction of a *potential psychic space* in his inner world.[17]

- In the history of the transference, we can (re)construct in a vivid way whether the patient believes or does not believe in psychic truths; we can also (re)construct how a potential psychic space is destroyed in the making; we can (re)construct essential unworded secrets.

Maybe we have a 'narcissistic father' in our psychic reality. Maybe we have a 'family romance' as well. It is certain that we are psychically organized by the Oedipal configuration. But the Oedipus myth tells us that if the parents relate to their offspring with a narcissistic filicidal hatred (or a narcissistic incestuous eroticization) instead of recognizing and containing intrapsychically their own unconscious desires and history; and if secrets concerning genealogy impinge on the family novel, trust in psychic truths can be destroyed and the essential Oedipal configuration that structures our mind, *perverted*. Maybe then the psychoanalytical working through of the oedipal conflicts is also linked to a (re)construction of these unworded agonies.

'LISTENING TO LISTENING' AND *APRÈS-COUP* (1993)★

This essay presents ideas, which I formulated in 1981, about a function per-formed by the analyst during the session, namely that of listening. Let us take up the main theoretical ideas by way of four propositions:

1 The first is that the patient *speaks and listens on the basis of his unconscious identifications*, which are a constituent part of his psyche.
2 The second concerns what the patient does with our interpretations: He listens to the analyst's silence and interpretations and *reinterprets them in accordance with his unconscious identifications*. These reinterpretations are in general kept in silence; the analyst then has difficulty in recognizing them unless he listens to them attentively. I consider that the *analyst's recognition* of the patient's reinterpretations is of decisive importance.
3 The third proposition concerns the meaning acquired by the interpretation following the patient's reinterpretation: It assumes a *retroactive meaning*, which depends on how the patient listened to it.
4 The fourth proposition relates to the complete cycle of the interpretation, which must include what the patient does with the interpretation and the analyst's search for the fate the patient has bestowed on it. In other words, the interpretative cycle does not end with the analyst's interpretation.[1]

Après-coup[2] (*Nachträglichkeit*)

If we can avoid the notion of a sequence of events in time shaped by a linear determinism we come closer to what I am trying to convey. Freud adopts a

---

★ Based on a lecture presented at the San Francisco Institute on 13 September 1993 and published in 1996.

dialectical approach to the patient's history in stating that the patient subjects the events of the past to subsequent (*nachträglich*) revision. In 1896 he wrote to Fliess: 'The material present in the form of memory traces [is] [. . .] subjected from time to time to a *re-arrangement* in accordance with fresh circumstances – to a *re-transcription*' (Freud 1896 [1950]: 233).

A radical distinction must be drawn between this dialectical conception of time and Jung's idea of 'retrospective fantasies'. According to the English translation of Laplanche and Pontalis, the fate of 'deferred revision' depends on 'whatever it has been impossible in the first instance to incorporate fully into a meaningful context' (1967: 112). The word 'deferred' merely denotes something put off to a later time and does not adequately express the idea of retroactivity and remodelling whereby new value is conferred on certain psychic contents. *Nachträglichkeit, après-coup*, is a fundamental psychoanalytical concept.

While this concept could be confined to the assignment of new meaning to memory traces, *I extend it to an operation of après-coup in the analytic relationship that consists of two inseparable phases, one of anticipation and another of retroaction. My aim is to show how this mechanism operates in analytic listening.*

From this point of view, even the most elementary sentence is submitted to the operation of *après-coup*: While we are uttering a sentence, we are already anticipating a significance that we do not yet clearly recognize and that is revealed to us retroactively. When we propose an interpretation, we anticipate a meaning that has not yet become quite clear and that the patient has been unable fully to incorporate into a meaningful context. It is the patient himself who, by listening to the interpretation, will activate in his psyche a meaningful *unconscious* context. In this way, the original meaning put forward by the analyst may well be *transformed*, thereby creating unexpected openings. I deduce that the meaningful context is not fully known to the analyst, neither is it known beforehand to the patient.

My hypothesis is that this meaningful context is *linked to the history of the patient's unconscious identifications*. Even when the patient listens carefully to the interpretations, he inevitably hears them in accordance with these unconscious identifications. While not overlooking the distinction between hearing and listening, I prefer to speak of the patient's 'listening'.

The patient reinterprets the interpretation and his response 'betrays' the way in which he has reinterpreted it. By listening to how the patient has listened to the interpretation the analyst is then able retroactively to assign a new meaning to what was said. As we know, to this function of the analyst, which enables him to assign a retroactive meaning to his interpretations, I have given the name of 'listening to [the patient's] listening'.

The operation of après-coup *(*Nachträglichkeit*) is involved in the function of 'listening to listening'*, since, first, the analyst listens to the movement of anticipation created by his own interpretation, then, second, he assigns to this interpretation a *retroactive meaning* (which arises from the way the patient listened to it).

Listening to silence

The analyst chooses either to remain silent or to interpret. Sometimes the patient also hears the analyst's silence as though it were speaking to him. For example, a patient may devote a substantial part of his session to an account of an achievement of which he is proud. He stops talking and the analyst remains silent. When he speaks again after a long silence, the patient remembers the criticisms made by his father who was never satisfied with anything done by his son. We may infer that the patient has been listening to the analyst's silence as a criticism, as if the analyst were saying: 'That is nothing to be proud of.' Through the function of 'listening to listening', we can recognize *who* the analyst is at this particular moment in the transference.

A misunderstanding

Let us briefly recall the main case (which was fully examined in Chapter 2) which lead me to think in terms of 'listening to listening', the case of Lise, who devoted large parts of her sessions to tell anecdotes concerning the ill treatment and misfortune to which she was exposed. One recurring theme concerned her father, whom she blamed for the unhappiness he caused whenever he was present. But the patient made a point of trying to get close to him: This always ended in conflict, with Lise feeling very unhappy.

In an interpretation I tried to establish links between these situations, to find a relationship between her unhappiness and an intrapsychic conflict and to help the patient and myself to explore *who* in the transference was this analyst who listened to the complaints. The interpretation, 'You can only talk to me about one possible father, who makes you unhappy, and yet you seek him out', was followed by a silence that gradually gave way to catastrophic anxiety. She was unable, during the session, or at subsequent sessions, to say what caused such anxiety.

I do not know whether I could have helped her to overcome her anxiety, but I should have intervened at least once more, saying, for example, 'I wonder what you heard in the interpretation that aroused so much anxiety in you, beyond what I actually said' or ' I believe that a catastrophic meaning lies hidden in my interpretation'. At the time, however, I considered that an interpretation ceased to be evaluated once it had been proposed. Not that I thought that my interpretation was 'the truth'. I thought then, as I think now, that an interpretation is a hypothesis. But I was not yet aware that every interpretation is transformed in the patient's mind wrought by an unconscious context. Neither was I aware that I was anticipating a meaning that was going to be reinterpreted retroactively and that I would need to exercise a function of listening combining this twofold process of *anticipation* and *retroactive meaning* (après-coup, nachträglich).

Only some years later was she able to take up that session again, giving two different versions of my interpretation: 'Do you remember that session when you said that I could only speak of my father *when* he made me unhappy?' (first version). 'Now I understand that I thought you were saying to me: "Let go of your father, *because* he only makes you unhappy"' (second version). 'It was as though my mother had won again. I felt desperate because I could not say how she had won.' As we know, the 'remembered' first version was created by her. (My original interpretation had been: 'You can only talk to me about one possible father, who makes you unhappy and *yet* you seek him out.')

The interpretation had anticipated a meaning that could only be understood retroactively when the patient's reinterpretation was spelt out. The *interpretation had been heard through her unconscious identification with a kind of internal mother who used incompatible arguments to dispossess her of a father.*

Considering that in my chosen perspective 'unconscious alienated identifications' have a history, I would say that the general line of my interpretative activity – and in particular 'listening to listening' – facilitate the discovery of *'who' is speaking, in a historical context.* The question of 'who' had the analyst been in the transference during that first session and what kind of transference prompted the catastrophic anxiety could only be answered *après-coup* when the patient was able to say how she had heard my interpretation.

A paradoxical transference

Some of my analysands wanted to turn themselves into the docile models of what they imagined to be my theoretical position – to which often they actually came quite close! (We must indeed beware of minimizing what they perceive of the analyst through his interpretations and his silences.) In those cases, the resulting narcissistic fascination was an obstacle for me in remaining in the listening position (a mixture of 'not-knowing' and 'curiosity' in which the unexpected may come to be heard) and in consequence conditions were lacking for surprise to signal psychoanalytical discovery.

I am always concerned about the analyst's possible intrusion giving rise to a further deprivation of the analysand's own psychic space, for example about the analyst's exercising the functions of appropriation and intrusion.

A patient, whom I shall call Ernest, attempted to please me by referring repeatedly to what he imagined to be my theoretical options. (As with others, he sometimes came close to recognizing them.) I tried to free his psychic space from his submission to a model by interpreting his dependence on what he imagined would interest me (and, we might add, would therefore arouse my interest in him – but I did not interpret this). He responded to my interpretation by an outburst of anxiety.

This anxiety, triggered by the very interpretation aimed at freeing him from this submission, was the sign of a radical break of any link with an object. The intersubjective analytical relationship, in turn, became profoundly involved in this total object loss. In a further interpretation, I attempted to re-establish the intersubjective relationship, so that it now became possible *to speak of the loss* of a link with the object. Yet I was faced with the difficult task of putting a name to this anxiety. I interpreted: 'Maybe you have heard me as though I were saying to you: "I do not accept, or do not recognize, the efforts that you are making to please me. Hence I do not recognize any value in you".'

This interpretation made it possible to re-establish the intersubjective analytical link and, consequently, to put an end to the nameless anxiety without however totally overcoming an atmosphere of mistrust. We then worked on the fact that the loss of certainty as to what interests me puts him in danger. We were thus able to discover simultaneously, patient and analyst, that at the beginning of the analysis the patient had felt the need to construct his own interpretations and had ended up mistrusting the analytical relationship because he had always been in a *paradoxical* dependence.

What does the paradoxical aspect of this dependence consist of? As any other child, the patient had had no choice but to depend on his parents because of his helplessness. But in this case, he had soon recognized the moments when his parents maintained a lasting investment in him and those when they suddenly lost interest in him. In other words, the child thus feels compelled to discover where the parents' narcissistic interests lie.[3]

Parents who operate by way of a narcissistic object regulation do not maintain an investment, sustained essentially *by love*, that takes into account the child's interests. Thus, because Ernest lived in a state of dependence on the parents who considered him as a narcissistic object, he had to be sure that the *conditions* for the dependence remained: For him, to acquire a certain self-sufficiency consisted in foreseeing their field of narcissistic interests. Insofar as it is the *child himself who has to ensure that the conditions for the effectiveness of his own dependence are maintained*, I describe this type of dependence as 'paradoxical'.

How can we listen to this paradoxical dependence, which is *inaudible* and which the patient activates and maintains unconsciously? When this kind of dependency is put into question by an interpretation and the patient feels that the relation with the analyst is in danger, *the paradoxical nature of the dependence may, under certain conditions, be put into words*.

Let us come back to my reinterpretation: 'Maybe you have heard me as though I were saying to you: "I do not accept, or do not recognize, the efforts that you are making to please me. Hence I do not recognize any value in you".'

This new interpretation marks the beginning of the work of reconstructing, in the transference, the paradoxical dependence that we have just been considering. The patient is searching for the slightest clue that will enable him to foresee the interests of the analyst and thereby to be sure that the latter will remain interested in him, in so far as he himself remains within the *narcissistic field of the analyst*.

When I note in my interpretation his submission to a model that he assumes to be mine, he reacts with catastrophic anxiety because the interpretation puts in danger the mode of relationship he is actively seeking to establish with me. He cannot imagine any other possible relationship: Either I accept the narcissistic fascination he proposes *or there is no longer any link between us*.

It is this dilemma that leads to nameless anxiety, to the extent that Ernest feels the intersubjective analytical relationship to be in danger. The value that the manifestation of his anxiety acquires in the analysis derives from the fact that it allows me to analyse the transferential actualization of the paradoxical dependency. Up to that moment, this dependence could not be verbalized. His words entailed an action, an acting out in the transference of his dependency. The perspective adopted here is the *transferential reconstruction of the infantile paradoxical dependency in relation to the narcissism of the internal parents*.

There is a danger that the analyst may become entangled in a reciprocal narcissistic fascination. For this reason, he should refrain from seeking a confirmation of his theoretical hypotheses, particularly when he considers that he has every right to expect it. Should these hypotheses be confirmed, the confirmation should surprise both the analyst and the analysand.

When interpreting absence, we must distinguish between the intersubjective relationship and the object relationship. The *psychic presence* of the analyst is of the utmost importance: It is a basic *condition for the interpretation of absence*. It is also the condition necessary for the transformation of the patient's psychic functioning and for allowing the unspoken to be said.

Two problems stimulate my reflection: The limits of what can be verbalized and the limits of a given patient's analysability. From my perspective, what the analyst cannot hear will contribute to leaving unspoken the 'unspeakable'. We shall leave open the question of whether the limits of analysability do or do not coincide with the limits of the speakable.

How may the transference neurosis be understood on the basis of this particular perspective? I have, up to now, concerned myself with a quite specific mode of functioning – the narcissistic functioning that might remain inaudible – and that aspect of the oedipal functioning that the patient's discourse may tend to disavow. What then may be proposed concerning the transference neurosis in patients who have been particularly subjected to parental narcissism?

Narcissistic resistances constitute the clinical expression of the 'narcissistic dimension' (*temps narcissique*) of the Oedipus. Narcissistic resistances stand forth in the examples I have presented since it is analysis of this dimension ('time') that helps to reveal – or indeed to constitute – the transference neurosis. We have seen that narcissistic resistances themselves have a history and it is precisely by recognizing this history as (re)constructed in the transference that these resistances may be overcome. By distinguishing the concept of defence from the concept of resistance, we can also distinguish character analysis from what is considered here to be a historicization of narcissistic resistances. Needless to say, this highly complex question remains open.

I discovered at the same time as one of my patients, how much his horror of unpredictability – of the surprise experienced when the unconscious speaks just as much as the anxiety aroused in him by my interpretations – was linked to his own basic psychic makeup: It is there that the strict analytical framework finds its place since his parents, in their relationship with him, were unpredictable; the analysis, in itself, was a distressing metaphor of this unpredictable relationship.

Another vignette

In her first interview, Kathy complained of intellectual inhibitions and spoke to me in a psychoanalytic jargon that appeared to convey her idea of 'what an analysis ought to be like'. This language, 'translated from the analytic', was interposed between us like a screen. Kathy did not give me an impression of helplessness but looked at me with a certain defiance. During the first year, her manner of speaking became one of the focal points of our work. She spoke to me in a hard, mechanical, cutting voice; the terms she used were predictable; and the distance and inauthenticity of her words confirmed my initial impression of a barrier, which excluded something that might be of value to her from the communication with me. Kathy said that she could not speak about certain things because, if she did, it would be like a transgression.

Surprisingly, she one day associated my interpretations concerning her anxiety about occupying 'secret places' with the fact that she had never had a room of her own. Although the family lived in a large house, Kathy had always slept in her parents' bedroom. She had never thought that this might be a problem. When she was five, her father had moved to another bedroom. From then on, Kathy had excitedly waited for the time when her mother would invite her to share her bed. Describing this situation to me, Kathy's voice was full of emotion and betrayed unwonted passion. Plainly, Kathy was for the first time sharing with me her secret garden and showing me that she could obtain what she wanted only in transgression. Only the transgressive pleasure appeared; the painful idea that she had no legitimate place did not occur to her conscious mind. This being the case, it is readily understandable how difficult it was for Kathy to acknowledge what she really wanted.

Her father always appeared as a distant, ascetic, intellectual figure, who had no contact with her (or with the mother). 'He was a real Robespierre, always cutting off people's heads', said Kathy. Let us see how this 'head-cutting father' appears in a session.

Kathy: In the last session, your interpretation was that I was claiming only to love M (a friend's wife) but that through a slip of the tongue I showed that I also felt hostile towards her. [She is very annoyed with me. The hostility appears in the transference. I wait.] It's true that, when I hid so many things from X, I was castrating him . . . But at least he listened to me, unlike my father, the dreaded Robespierre, who never listened to me or took any notice of me.

It seems to me that she *heard my interpretation* as a violent attack on her, perhaps I had not been listening to her: An analogue of the father, who perhaps cuts off people's heads . . . I continue to wait. With an object I cannot see, Kathy begins to make a metallic noise that punctuates her words: CLICK. I regard this as a symptomatic act (reminiscent of that of Dora). I wondered what relation this noise bears to her words and I listen as if to two interlaced musical themes:

Kathy: I remember this woman I had to see for my job . . . click . . . she had forgotten about me . . . click . . . it was very early in the morning . . . click . . . so I decide to seduce her instead of showing her how annoyed I was at her having forgotten me . . . click . . . so somehow in order to seduce her I pretended that she was someone who meant something to me . . . click . . . I suppose I put on an air of modesty for that reason . . . so that she should feel sorry for me . . . click . . . I think that it was a way of getting into her bed (thus seductively alluding to a previous interpretation of mine) . . . click . . . I think that good questions have answers that are not directly to the point, that work mainly through good associations . . . click . . . Then I had that other interview with the boss . . . click . . . he was very nice, though I was afraid that he would cut off my head as my father always did . . . click . . . '
Analyst: Yes, for a while now I have been hearing the noise of the guillotine.

In theoretical terms, Kathy may be said to be unconsciously identified with her 'head-cutting father'. Moreover, this identification is audible at this point in the session. Retroactively, I can *listen to her hard, metallic, cutting voice as equivalent to 'cutting off people's heads'*:

Kathy: What? [Surprise, silence.] . . . Oh yes, I see what you mean . . . the noise I was making with the clasp of my handbag! The guillotine . . . [in a contemptuous tone] . . . You might just as well have interpreted it as the coming together of the two parts of the clasp, as a love relation . . . [Changing her tone of voice.] Well, you're right . . . I wasn't aware of what I was doing . . . [Then in a cutting voice full of hate and defiance.] All right, if that's the way it is, I shall never again try to get a job!

Analyst: Since a head has been cut off, you feel tempted to share with me an interpretation of what we once said the interview meant for you. And since instead I spoke of the noise, does this mean that I am cutting off your head?

She did not say yes, but the tone of her voice changed in the last few minutes of the session. Let us now hear what Kathy says later, at another point in her analysis.

Yesterday I was so moved when I left . . . It was the first time that I had felt myself to be intelligent. I know that I can be unintelligent. I know that. But I am talking about a new feeling of being really intelligent. It was great, it was very exciting and, yes, moving . . . [Kathy is speaking in a soft voice, full of emotion, which I would describe as 'round' as opposed to her 'cutting' voice.] It is very important for me to have questioned the idea that my mother is perfect, incapable of making a mistake, as I have always told you. None of us could see her differently. I always considered that my mother was the most perfect and most seductive person in the world.

She talks of how she sees the sexuality of her mother and her own sexuality. Her voice then changes and takes on a more cutting, hard and mechanical tone:

My father never paid any attention to me. My four brothers thought I was clinging . . . And my mother . . . she never gave me any of her time either . . . except her precious time in bed . . . but she never took a minute of her time to listen to me . . . to find out what I was feeling or what I was thinking. You know, I never knew what my mother was really thinking. She was so false, so conventional, so seductive, I could never make contact with her real feelings and her real thoughts.

This was the first time Kathy had spoken of her mother as being false. She had often given me an impression of inauthenticity in the analysis. Then she returns to the subject of her sexuality:

All she wanted from me was a seductive appearance, as if what was inside, what a person feels or thinks, did not matter. If she had only taken the trouble to convey to me what she was thinking, instead of offering me only her body contact, which was so exciting . . . Well, I think my father was also partly to blame. He was incapable of forgiving, but always cutting off people's heads. Perhaps what my mother did was unforgivable. [She says what she thinks about what her mother did.] But it was not only a matter of forgiving or not forgiving. Instead of forgiving, my father cut off the relationship with his wife and ceased to be a husband. A few sessions ago, you said I could ask my friend to forgive me, because I had been able to forgive myself. I was always so arrogant towards her . . . It was very good that you recognized that.

Her voice changes again, back to its cutting and metallic form, full of hate:

In old times I would have let myself be cut into tiny pieces rather than confess and express my regret. I always lied. [Silence.] Now I should like you to tell me what you think and to say whether my associations are correct . . . [Silence.]

This is a typical situation in which she tries to push me into doing certain things and then her voice becomes cutting and full of hate:

Analyst: It must be hard for you to accommodate a new situation inside yourself. You were forging links between your ideas and your words, thinking, having new feelings . . . and all of a sudden your voice changes. It feels like you are trying to force me to say something so as to make us share the same opinion, the same bed. Perhaps now, at the end of the session, you are seeking a particular contact, trying to obtain certain words as if they were bodily contact.

Kathy: [The patient's tone of voice changes again as she says reflectively] Perhaps I can now start thinking that I can do without . . . this.

Après-coup

Finally, if my proposed dialectical concept of time, in which a text retroactively takes on a meaning in accordance with a specific context, is applied to the reading of this essay, each reader will perhaps draw a different conclusion according to his particular psychoanalytic culture. I have presented here a number of interrelated themes, so that it is not easy to predict the resonances that will be aroused in each reader by these themes, individually or in combination. However, I should not like this idea to leave us in an ambiguous position. Although some of this essay's conclusions are open ended, that does not mean that they lack a precise objective. My principal justification for the concept of 'listening to listening' is that the patient interprets on different levels of meaning.

Again, the narcissistic transference becomes analysable provided that it is listened to. I shall confine myself here to drawing certain conclusions applicable to a single standpoint, that of listening to the fate of the interpretation and its connection with the concept of *après-coup*, *Nachträglichkeit*.

An interpretation entails at least two logical phases of understanding, the first concerns the analyst and the second depends on the patient. The analyst anticipates a meaning on the basis of the transference history and this also involves his countertransference position. By virtue of a complex constellation of factors, the analyst, in part, chooses the formulation and in part is led to it. The patient speaks and listens in accordance with his unconscious identifications, as a result of which he reinterprets the analyst's interpretations. This hypothesis leads us to see the interpretation of misunderstanding as the royal road to the discovery of these identifications.

In addition to the meaning opened up by the interpretation and the (après-coup) reattribution of meaning by the patient, there is a third logical phase, that of comparison of the two forms of expression, which leads both to the retroactive meaning of the interpretation and to understanding the unconscious identification. In this phase, the analyst is able to formulate a reinterpretation that takes account of this new meaning. The function of 'listening to listening' has another consequence: In listening to how the analyst has heard him, the patient gradually acquires the capacity to listen to himself.

In this way, we may hope to overcome the dilemma that would arise if we were to ask 'who is right, the analyst or the patient?'. By the function of 'listening to listening', we try to tune into the speaking of the unconscious and each of its vicissitudes.

MISUNDERSTANDING AND
PSYCHIC TRUTHS (1995)*

Introduction

I shall refer throughout this essay to the concept of *après-coup* (*Nachträglichkeit*, 'deferred action' according to Strachey), which entails the twin elements of anticipation and retroactive meaning. I hope that the reader too, by a similar retroactive process, will find that new light has been cast on what is already known about psychic reality and, thereby, links will have been forged between the concepts of psychic reality, historical truths and psychic truths, on the one hand, and those of decentred listening and misunderstanding, on the other. In proposing the concepts of 'decentred listening' and of 'listening to listening', I wish to add a new dimension to the already familiar notions of evenly suspended attention and free association.

'Someone is speaking to someone'; 'someone is listening to someone'; 'someone is reading someone': From my chosen perspective, this listening and this reading are already interpretations. In an analysis, both the analysand and the analyst are speaking about something that is absent from the point of view of material reality. This absent object is a psychoanalytic psychic object. In the session, for example, we interpret not a dream, which is an absent object, but the *account* of a dream, which forms part of the context of the history of the transference. The account is communicated to someone – that is to say, it has an addressee in the transference. We may recall that Freud once interpreted to one of his woman patients that the wish fulfillment in her dream was to demonstrate that Freud was wrong, that the theory of dreams as wish fulfillment was incorrect. The patient's unconscious wish was to thwart Freud's wish.

* This version was written for the opening session of the 39th International Psychoanalytical Congress in San Francisco on 31 July 1995, which was read in an abridged version. This chapter is the complete version published in English in 1997.

I shall now put forward my central thesis. It is that the *concept of psychic reality raises a problem concerning the status assignable to the subject's history and to material reality. There is solipsism here, in that only the subject is deemed to exist or be knowable.* I shall put forward a theoretico-clinical proposition that might enable us to attribute a psychoanalytic status to the history of the subject and hence to overcome this kind of solipsism. I have already considered this issue in earlier writings (and, particularly in Chapter 6).

Freud's discovery and psychic reality

The concept of psychic reality is pivotal to Freud's conceptualization of psycho-analysis. Indeed, for some schools it may be said to lie at the very heart of psychoanalysis. As with any concept, it is appropriate to examine how the concept of psychic reality came to be formulated in the history of psychoanalytic ideas. A concept cannot be regarded as an initial given that never needs to be reconsidered.

Let us begin by recalling Freud's question about why the seduction scene seems real to the patient if in most cases it never occurred in material reality. Unconscious wishes and unconscious fantasies produce *real effects*.[1] Freud's novel concept of psychic reality thus manages to avoid all idealism: Every unconscious wish (both the unconscious wish and its fantasy elaboration) is therefore deemed real.

Here I shall not refer to the unconscious fantasy or wish as such. Following Freud, I shall speak of psychic reality, while emphasizing its unconscious dimension. Freud considered that both material and psychic reality were real in the sense that he acknowledged the power of the unconscious scene to produce real effects.

Freud had already begun to give an implicit reply to the question of the reality status of the seduction scene when he wrote in 1895: 'Indications of discharge through speech are also in a certain sense indications of reality – *but of thought–reality, not of external reality*' (Freud 1895: 373 (emphasis added))

It may be noted in passing that, at the very moment when he was sketching out the concept of psychic reality ('thought–reality'), Freud connected it with the notion of language:

> The unconscious is the true psychical reality: *In its innermost nature it is as much unknown to us as the reality of the external world, and it is as incompletely presented by the data of consciousness as is the external world by the communications of our sense organs.*
>
> (Freud 1900: 613 (emphasis added))

Again, Freud assigned equivalent status to the concepts of external reality and material reality. This equivalence can be observed throughout his *oeuvre* and the theoretico-clinical problems it raises are so important and interesting that they should be studied in their own right:

> Whether we are to attribute *reality* to unconscious wishes, I cannot say. It must be denied, of course, to any transitional or intermediate thoughts. If we look at unconscious wishes reduced to their most fundamental and truest shape, we shall have to conclude, no doubt, that *psychical* reality is a particular form of existence not to be confused with *material* reality. [Strachey notes that this sentence, added in 1914, ended with the words 'factual reality' and that 'material reality' was substituted in 1919.]
>
> (Freud 1900: 620)

This conception of Freud's brings psychoanalysis close to the realm of phenomenology, because he is here using the device of *epochè* in regard to the material reality of the event. Concerning the concept of psychic reality, I propose to examine the following theoretico-clinical question: *Under what conditions can the concept of psychic reality be deemed to retain its psychoanalytic relevance?* After all, Freud bases the concept precisely on his suspension of judgement about material reality. The criteria that distinguish psychoanalysis from phenomenology are the concept of the unconscious and psychoanalytic listening. The latter is *not* centred on consciousness: To emphasize the difference, I use the term 'decentred listening'.

Freud, of course, relinquished neither the concept of the unconscious nor the psychoanalytic method after his methodological and ethical integrity led him to confess (both to himself and to Fliess) that he no longer believed in his 'neurotica' (Freud 1897: 264–6).

The theoretical concept of the unconscious and the psychoanalytic method for discovery of the unconscious dimension are, in my view, the necessary (not sufficient) *conditions for qualifying the concept of psychic reality as psychoanalytic.*

Pre-Freudian criteria of objectivity for the appreciation of reality are overturned. The suspension of judgement about material reality provides us with another criterion of objectivity for the purpose of inferring psychic reality while allowing for intersubjectivity, because the 'other' is present from the beginning in the constitution of psychic reality. Reality is initially mediated by the explicit and implicit parental discourse, including the unconscious dimension of the parents' psyche, as Laplanche (1987) recalls.

Objectivity arises within intersubjectivity. This intersubjectivity is a trans-ference dimension whereby we can reconstruct the intrasubjective, intrapsychic aspect of the *unconscious* conflict. The intersubjective relationship reveals the intrasubjective relationship and allows a different solution to the unconscious intrapsychic conflict. There is therefore *something pre-existing* to be discovered, reconstructed, even constructed, created – for transference entails not only repetition but also transformation, creation.

Decentred listening

I suggest that psychic reality be *inferred* in the intrasubjective dimension of the unconscious conflict through an intersubjective transference function in the analysis, namely, that of listening to listening, as I have called it since 1981. We infer psychic reality by listening to listening. The patient's psychic reality can be deduced from the distance between what the analyst thinks he has interpreted and what the patient actually heard. In this function of listening to listening, *new meaning is to be assigned retroactively (nachträglich)* to the interpretation. In this sense, misunderstanding becomes the key to the discovery of psychic reality in terms of its truth-creating effects: We may speak of psychic *truths*. It is not a matter of the 'Truth'. However, this applies *only* to *certain* forms of misunderstanding.

I postulate that the function of listening to listening is *one* of the criteria whereby psychic reality and its truth-creating effects can be evaluated. *Far from constituting a mere technical device, this function is consistent with my perception of the formation of the psyche, because the other is present from the beginning in the constitution of psychic reality.*

If asked why I would rather speak of decentred listening than of evenly suspended listening and free association, I would answer that the question leaves aside precisely the dimension I wish to add to the classical concepts. The kind of listening I am proposing entails:

- Listening out for how the patient hears the analyst's interpretations or silences ('listening to listening').
- Retroactively assigning meaning to the analyst's interpretations and silences on the basis of this listening to listening.
- Allowing the process of listening to listening to appear in the interpretation.
- Ensuring that the patient can listen to the way the analyst listens to him so that he can become able to listen to himself: We shall then have two subjects whose listening is decentred.

I contrast this notion of decentred listening with a form of introspection that is centred on consciousness and makes no use of the concept of the unconscious.

The analyst's psychic reality

In discussing the psychic reality of the analyst, I must reaffirm that his psychic functioning too includes an unconscious dimension – which is not necessarily synonymous with neurosis. Some authors disregard the psychic functioning of the analyst in the study of the transference and its interpretation. Others, apparently following Annie Reich, acknowledge the analyst's unconscious psychic activity only through his symptoms and see it in terms solely of his neurosis (see Chapter 4). However, if the psychic dimension of the analyst is excluded, an objectifying attitude is liable to be adopted towards the patient. If the patient is seen as an object, the analyst becomes a mere external observer.

I agree with many authors[2] in that the analyst is not an observer external to the analytic process: Relative to another subject (the patient) and in a dissymmetrical position, he intervenes with his own psychic functioning (including its unconscious dimension), his theory, the transference relationship he had with his own analyst, his supervisions, his theoretical allegiance and so on. Other studies take account of the psychic dimension of the analyst, but in an introspective form. In these cases, the analyst focuses on his own psychic processes and, putting himself in a subjectivistic position, analyses his own psychic field. In this way, in subtle accounts of psychic functioning reminiscent of the phenomenological descriptions of a Merleau-Ponty, the unconscious dimension tends to become blurred because the emphasis is on the field of consciousness (albeit widened).

The subjectivism I have just described may have arisen in response to the problems raised by (a) the objectifying position referred to earlier; (b) a reductionist vision of psychoanalysis; or (c) a certain kind of analysis in which the analyst puts himself in the position of a person who has already understood everything and is merely biding his time until the appropriate moment arrives for him to apply his theory.

My chosen theoretico-clinical point of view presupposes that (a) an intrasubjective conflict is recreated in the transference in the intersubjective relationship between patient and analyst; (b) the intrasubjective conflict is thus discovered in the patient; and (c) the analyst as a subject himself takes account of his own psychic functioning, that is, of his own unconscious psychic reality (and of its possible effects on the analytic process).

The analyst, in a dissymmetrical position and following the personal working through of his conflicts, places his psyche in the service of understanding that of the patient. It is from this countertransference position that the analyst assumes the function of listening to listening, that is, of discovering the patient's psychic reality and of retroactively understanding *who* the analyst is in the transference (by taking account of the gulf between what he thought he said and what the patient actually heard).

In our role of accompanying the patient, we discover with him the actual nature of his psychic reality, which is, of course, unconscious. This discovery is a surprise to analyst and patient alike. In other words, it is not a matter of imposing on the patient the psychic reality we ascribe to him. Whatever precautions we take, it sometimes happen – more often than we care to admit – that we find in the patient only what we have previously attributed to him and leave aside what does not confirm our expectations. From this point of view, the work of countertransference analysis also entails overcoming the tautology

91

of listening only to what we have already taken into account on the basis of our theories.

A paradoxical dimension of psychic reality

I do not by any means consider that psychoanalytic listening is a 'natural' kind of listening. I agree with those analysts who believe that theory plays an active part in the construction of the psychoanalytic object and that our listening depends on a complex dialectic constellation. In the examples I present, my listening is underlain by certain concepts (among others) developed by myself in previous writings (and which now constitute the different chapters in the current volume). That said, I should now like to focus on a major problem on the patient's side that may in my view arise at certain points in any analysis.

To remain for the time being on the conceptual level before embarking on the clinical examples, we observe that some patients present *an inherently paradoxical psychic reality to which they deny a psychic character and which thus carries within itself a disavowal. Such patients put forward this reality not as their own but as belonging to a world regarded as 'natural', which is therefore reified. The patient cannot see himself as the subject of this reality and does not recognize its psychic nature* (Faimberg 1973).

In this form of resistance, he refuses to acknowledge his intrapsychic conflicts and the dimension of otherness proper to the unconscious; this reality is presented as beyond his reach. *Unheimlich* is the word used by Freud to denote the uncanny otherness that is the hallmark of the unconscious (Freud 1919b).

In my view, this paradoxical aspect (that of psychic reality unrecognized as such) may appear in *any* analysis at a point in the history of the transference when the patient fails to acknowledge the intrapsychic and unconscious value of the transference conflict. It may be objected that it is illegitimate to speak of psychic reality if the patient does not recognize it. However, I hope that this essay will indicate the value of including even this type of functioning within the concept of psychic reality. After all, when a patient is unable to acknowledge his psychic reality, he cannot acknowledge his psychic *responsibility* towards his unconscious. Psychic responsibility begins when the patient succeeds in seeing himself as the subject of his psychic functioning, that is, in recognizing his unconscious psychic reality. This recognition implies that psychic reality has real consequences in the intrapsychic and intersubjective links discovered by the patient in his analysis. Psychic responsibility must be distinguished from narcissistic omnipotence.

Decentred listening: Inferring psychic reality

Maryse did not accept my interpretations of her psychic reality. For her the world was organized as if it were natural and she was unable to see herself as its subject. In what she said, she did not recognize herself as a psychically responsible subject.

'My father never counted in my life. Only my mother counted, with her cold and scornful gaze', says Maryse in a cold and scornful voice. For her, 'this' father (whom I interpret as part of her psychic reality) *is* reality. She accepts no psychic responsibility for 'this inexistent father'. Sometimes, in a warmer tone, she uses popular sayings that we discover are favourite expressions of the father. Through my decentred listening I hear Maryse's father speaking (where neither she nor I are expecting it).

What father do we talk about once we have suspended judgement about material reality? This father takes shape through what the analysand says and cannot say, according to her psychic reality.

After Maryse has quoted one of these proverbs in a session, I interpret: 'Your father often talks to us through these sayings. Have you any idea what makes you think that he never existed in your life?'[3]

This question addresses an enigmatic aspect of the transference. I do not expect from Maryse a reply resulting from conscious introspection: I am helping her to listen in a decentred way to 'her–his' discourse and to recognize the intrapsychic character of this symbolic father who *does* exist. I am helping her to listen to the two different discourses she is expressing – 'her words/her father's words' and 'my father never counted in my life' and to recognize an intrapsychic conflict.

When Maryse denied her father's place in her life, my interpretations about his actual place were experienced as intrusive because they brought her back to the father she *ought* to have had but who did not concern *her*. The comment 'My father never counted in my life' can now be interpreted as an expression of her wish, namely that only her mother should matter.

With the analysis of her unconscious homosexuality, she was able to tell me that her mother had suggested that they should adopt a baby together. The status of this mother (the one who suggested the adoption) raises a genuine problem, because certain parents of the patient's psychic reality cannot be regarded as imagos resulting solely from the projection of the child's wishes; in the present case, Maryse's homosexual wishes. Let us confine ourselves for the time being to drawing attention to the problem of solipsism.

Beyond Maryse's conscious representation of the father's role, decentred listening enabled us to gain access to her unconscious psychic reality. In the psychic reality thus discovered, we can recognize the symbolic function of the father: Maryse acknowledges at one and the same time her own psychic reality and the symbolic role of her father.

Decentred listening (on the part of both analyst and patient) enables us to analyse how Maryse places herself as the subject of her psychic reality and to overcome the paradox mentioned earlier.

Listening to misunderstanding: *Who* is speaking?

Here is another vignette to illustrate my concepts; it includes an initial interpretation that I do not consider appropriate. The patient, Brigitte, talks once again in a provocative and apparently unemotional way of various sexual relationships in which she tries to get herself pregnant as though she does not care who the baby's father might be. She imagines that I shall use a theory about the importance of the father that will lead me to moralize; she refers to situations that smell bad; the bad smell of her last partner; if it were not for the smell she would have a child with him. She adds, sarcastically, that it is perhaps merely a question of finding some good deodorant. A silence then ensues.

I felt that if I kept silent she would hear my silence as a collusion with someone in her psychic reality totally indifferent to her suffering and despair. I had difficulty in finding an interpretation and, with hindsight, I think that this is precisely what I ought to have interpreted, that is, the fact that she was talking to me as if I were someone completely indifferent to her suffering and despair. However, my actual interpretation was as follows:

> *Analyst*: You talk about situations characterized by a bad smell and about your intention to get pregnant; as though you felt there is a link between the two situations and as if you were saying that something in this project seems to smell bad.
> *Brigitte*: You have no right to say that *and* I'd very much like to insult you.

I then said to her:

> *Analyst*: You said with anger '*and* I want to insult you' . . . This '*and*' [I want to insult you] makes me think that you heard my interpretation as though it were an insult.

We (the patient and myself) listen retroactively (*nachträglich*) to the way she heard the interpretation. Once again, I interpret in hypothetical form. I could have expressed myself more concisely, omitting the first, descriptive part in which I quote her words. However, she tends to expel explosively everything that causes her anxiety and it seemed important to me to give her enough time to place herself in a listening position. Perhaps I suspected that in her 'talion logic' she might hear this fresh interpretation as a sequence of mutual insults. I therefore formulate the interpretation slowly and in a reflexive style that complements[4] her explosive–expulsive reply. I am trying to establish in Brigitte a kind of decentred listening, so that she can listen to my way of listening and thereby become capable of listening to herself. I am trying to forge an intersubjective (transferential) link so as to bring out an intrasubjective link. For the time being, the interpretation has been heard as an attack:

> *Brigitte*: It's not a matter of what I heard, what you actually said was: 'Tell me about your projects: You can only produce foul-smelling projects' [in a contemptuous and dismissive voice that creates an enigma in me].

Until now, I thought I had failed to create the virtual space of the patient's unconscious psychic reality, because she says that what she heard is actually what I said – as if there could be no discrepancy between what I said and what she heard. In the transference relationship, which is intersubjective, the patient listens to my interpretation from the standpoint of a psychic reality *not yet recognized as such*. We shall discover it together by following the vicissitudes of 'listening to listening'.

The words that were equivalent to actions (insults) are beginning to find expression: We have different discourses to compare. By 'discourse', I mean here the discourse of a patient, with his suffering, history and transference relationship, the analysis of which cannot be confused with that of a literary text, as Green (1973) aptly pointed out. Again, this equivalence between words and actions should be understood in terms of the concept for which Freud used the German word *agieren* (to act out):

> *Analyst*: Through my interpretation, it is possible that we – you and I – are hearing someone who treats you as if you were worthless. If so . . . , I wonder who that might be?

I formulate the first part of my interpretation hypothetically, referring to someone impersonal speaking through the mouth of the analyst. In this way I implicitly point to the patient's psychic reality. We – she and I – need to find out whether the psychic reality I infer – through listening to listening – is in fact hers at this point in the transference. In formulating the question 'Who might that someone be?' I am using a rhetorical style that does not call for a conscious answer but awaits an opening, an *unconscious association*. Here are her unconscious associations:

> *Brigitte*: [In my adolescence . . .] Mother told me that I should look after my teeth as daughters inherit their father's teeth. I protested that we both had good teeth. Before leaving the room, my mother, as though it were of no importance, declared that my father was not my real biological father. When, later, I could ask for explanations, she told me that I was making a

fuss about nothing. She told me that my father had recognized me so that she would not have an abortion.

Through her association with the story of her parentage, Brigitte confirms that my reinterpretation is in resonance with her psychic reality. The question has to do with the transference conflict and the unconscious associations (to the enigma in the transference) and not with introspection and the conscious answers. The story told by Brigitte is the unconscious response she tries to give to this enigma, with the retroactive assignment of new meaning: This psychic reality stems partly from Brigitte's unconscious identification with 'that mother' who rejects her daughter and pays no attention to her as a person, as if her revelation were of absolutely no consequence. In theoretico-clinical terms, it may be added that in the patient's psychic reality she is identified to a phallic mother who exercises omnipotent power. By unforeseeable intrusions, she appropriates her daughter's identity and parentage without the slightest regard for the psychic suffering she is inflicting on her.

Why does Brigitte listen to the interpretation as having no other possible meaning than that she is a 'worthless person', capable only of 'foul-smelling projects?' It is *because Brigitte listens to my interpretation through the unconscious identification with the mother*. In the transference relationship, we succeeded in recognizing this type of mother in the way the patient heard my interpretation – *as if the analyst's words were those of her mother*.

The psychic reality is revealed in the patient's way of listening to the interpretation. In other words, we recognized this type of mother in the *inter*subjective relationship. However, the way the patient listened to the interpretation is *also rooted in a historical truth*. That is to say, Brigitte's psychic reality is connected with a certain historical truth. I suggest that we should here be talking about *psychic truths*. I shall return to this point later.

Retroactively, I recognize the violent, detached voice of the mother in the patient's tone. We discover that the tone of voice used by the patient to tell me how she heard my interpretation coincides with that of the omnipotent mother. Why do I not now simply say that the patient is speaking (or that I am interpreting), rather than that 'that mother' (the mother of the patient's psychic reality) is speaking (intrapsychically or through what the analyst says)? It is because I wish to emphasize the *patient's unconscious identification with an 'other', which is a constitutive part of her psyche*. We are talking about the identification with her mother's discourse.

The *intra*subjective reference is intended to stress that there is always an 'other' to be discovered in the patient's psychic reality. I trust that this view will not be misinterpreted as a reification of the psyche or as an anthropomorphism, as if I were thinking of a kind of stage character ensconced inside the psyche. As stated, what I am referring to is the unconscious identification with the *discourse* of an other (with what is spoken *and* unspoken).

During the same session, I was able to connect this historical truth with the unconscious transference conflict by means of the following interpretation:

Analyst: By telling me about your efforts to get pregnant, perhaps you were trying to explore what are you entitled to, what is a legitimate desire and who confers legitimacy.
Brigitte: My father saved my life, and he's my real dad.

This raises a theoretical question: Given that it is the patient who tells the story (and, as the psychoanalytic method demands, only she must tell it), in what respects is this story unconscious? What is unconscious is the *link* between her words and the way these words concern *her*. She is not aware of the links between her words and her intrapsychic (intrasubjective) conflict, which is triggered by the enigma of the transference (the intersubjective relationship).

Moreover, her refusal to let me interpret something in terms of 'a father' was also based on a historical truth: She presumed that I would talk about 'this father' from the point of view of *my* theory and without concern for her (in the same way as this mother had spoken of her parentage, that is, without attaching the slightest importance to it and taking no notice of her as a person).

Psychic responsibility and historical truths

However, one essential component is lacking in our analysis, namely that of the patient's responsibility for her own psychic functioning, her own psychic reality and her unconscious wishes, which are always *active*. It is not only a matter of discovering the patient's psychic reality but also of helping her to see herself as *a subject relative to that reality*. That is what we call *responsibility* for one's own *unconscious* conflicts.

In the session, I initially left the still undecided status of 'this mother' in abeyance. As we know, if we suspend judgement on the materiality of the events on which the patient's psychic reality is based, psychic reality inevitably falls prey to a certain solipsism (Cahn 1991). I think that, as analysts, we need to contain in our psyche the uncertainty resulting from this position. It must be accepted that this somewhat solipsistic solution was necessary to resolve a dilemma that would have destroyed the very foundations of psychoanalysis as a unique and original field of knowledge. This vignette illustrates the importance of suspending judgement on the material status of the object (*epochè*).

However, I have had occasion elsewhere (in particular, in Chapters 5 and 6) to study the psychic status of parents and have argued that we must not always assume that some parent figures are nothing but projection products of the patient's aggression in oedipal rivalry. This is illustrated by the mother, who suggests to Maryse that they should adopt a baby together. I have also said that, in the reconstruction based on the history of the transference and in the strict setting of the treatment, we can infer what type of parents the patient might have had, even though this inference can only ever be hypothetical.

In the session just discussed, the patient allows us to hear a type of mother who reveals her daughter's paternal parentage in disavowal, in a trivializing tone that takes no account of the anxiety she is arousing in her daughter.

This trivializing, contemptuous discourse of the mother's reappears in my patient *when she interprets what I have told her* ('you can only produce foul-smelling projects'). Given that she ascribes a trivializing tone to my interpretation, I preferred to interpret, *first of all, this type of mother as the one who was speaking in the transference.* In other words, as we have seen, the patient hears my interpretation from the position of her identification with that mother. This means that we grasped her unconscious identification with this type of mother in the way the interpretation was listened to. Here the *unconscious psychic reality* is revealed in *inter*subjectivity.

It was, at the same time, important that I accepted the fact that this mother was actually speaking through my interpretation, because, if I had over-hastily said, 'It is your intrapsychic mother who is speaking', that would have reactivated the *disavowal* (*Verleugnung*) of her own psychic suffering. She would have heard: 'It is not true that you had that mother, who spoke to you in a cruel and trivializing tone about your parentage: That mother exists *only* in your mind.' In that case, the introduction of the psychic reality would for her have had the *opposite* meaning to that of the historical truth.

Now it is both theoretically and clinically desirable for us to establish a dialectic between the concept of unconscious psychic reality and that of historical truth. Our example illustrates the kernel of historical truth mentioned by Freud (1937: 269).

However, I had to recognize with my patient the *consequences* of this type of mother in her *intra*psychic (*intra*subjective) and *inter*psychic (*inter*subjective) links and, hence, her psychic responsibility. In another session we again encounter the mother's style, as already recognized, when the patient criticizes an interpretation and trivializes it with a harsh tone. I then tell her that she is stripping all legitimacy from what concerns us (both herself and me) in the session (like this mother we have recognized, who strips all value from legitimacy, as if it were something that simply did not matter).

It is the discovery of the unconscious identification with a type of mother *in a historical context* that now allows the patient to determine her *position* with respect to her own psychic reality and her historical truths. In this way, she was able to hear an interpretation of the transference and become responsible for her unconscious conflicts and their consequences. In other words, she was able to hear an interpretation about the responsibility she bore for her own psychic reality and history.

Having thus determined the field of her psychic responsibility, she was able to make due allowance for certain historical truths for which she was *not* responsible and to establish her position as the subject of her psychic truths. *Misunderstanding eventually enabled us to discover her unconscious psychic truths.*

Can she now construct a reliable relationship in her psychic reality and is she now more able to believe in the value of psychic truths?

Overcoming solipsism: Psychic realities and historical truths

An enigma emerges in the transference at the parting of the ways between what the analyst says and what the patient hears. What is it in the patient that determines the choice between different versions? Everything depends on *who* is speaking (for the patient) through the analyst's interpretation; this is ultimately a matter of the patient's psychic reality. Given that the patient, in unconsciously attempting to resolve this enigma, is led to tell something about his history or his parents' history, his account may be regarded as *one of the possible versions of the historical truths.* For this reason, we must preserve the psychoanalytic conditions necessary for the discovery of truths in order to guarantee that the history belongs to the patient's psyche and to maintain the distinction between information and history. The history *is not a pre-existing given*, but is constructed gradually during the course of the analysis. While also emphasizing this distinction, Viderman (1970) explains (from a different position) in his remarkable book, *La Construction de l'Espace Analytique*, why he believes that this solipsism is unavoidable. I refer to psychic *truths* to show the connection between psychic *reality* and *historical* truths.

Psychic truths are the consequence of the psychic work resulting from the demands of reality that are fashioned by the unconscious wish and the unconscious fantasy. For this reason, the (re)construction of an infantile sexual theory is a version of the psychic truths.

The status of the object is also involved, as witness the mother who suggests to Maryse that they adopt a baby and Brigitte's mother who reveals with disavowal (of the suffering it causes) the parentage of her daughter. In view of the concept of psychic truths – we may imagine that 'those mothers' – cannot be regarded either as imagos resulting *solely* from the projection of the child's wishes or *solely* as the consequence of an infantile sexual theory. An insistent residue, a dimension of the 'real', remains. Moreover, as we have seen throughout this essay, the object concerned is a *historical* one.

My viewpoint is based *not* on the correspondence between psychic reality and material reality (or lack of it). Thus it is *not for the analyst to impose an adaptation to his own implicit or explicit criteria about reality*; these may be very unreal to the patient when he is living in a different psychic reality. This is a thorny problem because, as we have seen, a natural way of listening does not exist. The analyst's capacity to listen from a position of not-knowing (Bion 1967; Green 1989) and to contain nameless anxiety partially guarantees that the (re)construction of historical truths is not a mere intrusion of the analyst's theory.

In conclusion, within a non-linear system of causality, we retroactively and fragmentarily link together different psychic realities with versions of historical truths. *What allows solipsism to be overcome is the connection between psychic realities and historical truths, and hence the concept of psychic truths.* The function of listening to listening allows us to analyse misunderstanding, which is the *via regia* to the discovery of psychic truths.

NARCISSISTIC DISCOURSE AS A RESISTANCE TO PSYCHOANALYTICAL LISTENING:★ A CLASSIC SUBMITTED TO THE TEST OF IDOLATRY (2001)

When considering idolization I do not speak about idols established and widely recognized as such, but about the use to which we may at some point put a text, an idea, a fragment of truth, a particular conception of our work. Unconsciously aimed at organizing our identity, this process has the consequence of creating an idol and becomes a resistance to analytic listening and to the dialogue between analysts.

An analyst who has in this way organized his affiliation to an aspect of theory may think, when listening to a colleague who expresses ideas different to the ones he upholds, "This issue has already been solved by X (his chosen author)". But this does not require that the (preferred) author be an established idol or that he has actually adopted a totalitarian discourse.

In this presentation, I shall exclusively consider the narcissistic resistances to analytic listening. Under the effect of narcissistic discourse and narcissistic listening, the criteria of pleasure–unpleasure prevail in varying degrees over the remaining criteria applied to the discovery of truths.

Let us see once again one of the possible ways in which the human being negotiates unpleasure. In narcissistic discourse,[1] the subject speaks of the world as if it were a natural given, he reifies it and limits himself to asserting that the world *is*, without feeling any obligation to recognize his own possible psychic *responsibility for its meaning*. Such a discourse deserves to be called narcissistic

★ First presented at the European Psychoanalytical Federation Conference, Madrid, April 2001.

because its function is to preserve the narcissistic cohesion (and sometimes even the psychic survival) of the person who utters it. Because of this narcissistic regulation, the subject does not easily localize the causes of his pleasure or unpleasure. The aim of this regulation is to abolish the degree of psychic responsibility he has in his relationship to the world. It is inherent in the narcissistic organization that the subject prefers any discourse that designates the other as the origin of unpleasure and pain, and oneself as the origin of pleasure and well-being.

Narcissistic discourse negotiates pleasure–unpleasure in the following way: That which gives pleasure belongs to 'us', that which evokes unpleasure belongs to 'them'.

The reunification ideal constituent of narcissistic discourse is personified by the idol: It is he who determines what is designated as 'friendly' or 'enemy'. Thus narcissistic discourse implies an *anonymous subject devoid of psychic responsibility*. What is pleasure for one agency may be unpleasure for another: The discovery of this type of conflict and its working through in psychoanalytic listening, which form the basis of our daily work, will not be examined here.

I shall refer to those situations that, threatening the analyst's 'being', induce him to adopt for reasons of self-preservation a narcissistic mode of listening and/or a narcissistic discourse. It is sometimes difficult to discern why we, as analysts, think as we do, and where the ideas that we uphold come from. Certain types of discourse (whether in the mouth of the patient or in the mouth of a colleague) may create anxiety by arousing in us an unconscious fear of putting at risk a particular analytic filiation (explicit or implicit). And since our analytic filiation incorporates our transferential links, it is inevitably related to the roots of our analytic being.

Here I would like to refer to Ronald Britton's fine paper (1998) on publication anxiety. Among other interesting remarks, Britton mentions the case of Darwin, who ran the risk of not being recognized as the originator of his discoveries through long hesitating to publish them, afraid as he was of being banished from the scientific community.

Our wish to be attached to a psychoanalytical filiation is legitimate. If we are the children of nobody, we may fall prey to the dangerous fantasy of being self-begotten. Between the Charybdis of a filiation that could be taken as submission to a totalitarian discourse (and to an idol) and the Scylla of being nobody's child, we seek our true way as analysts. We may be tempted to adopt an idol when looking for a narcissistic solution to the many uncertainties that surround the process of becoming an analyst. If the idols we adopt are real thinkers, and are not willing to accept this kind of idolization, we still need to have a democratic dialogue within the psychoanalytical institution. I am speaking of how best we may achieve this particular blend of free spirit and rigorous intellect that would be most conducive to psychoanalytical listening.

A problem arises when, by adopting an authoritarian approach to discussion, the institution seems to confirm that narcissistic discourse is *the* way to belong to a group. In these circumstances, the idea of listening to something new both in theory and in the patient's discourse creates for the analyst a potential conflict with the group. The spectre of a solitude more radical than the solitude that we necessarily have to assume creates the conditions for the analyst to play his part in unconsciously transmitting to successive generations an attitude of submission to idols. Having said this, I do not forget that analysing the obstacles that interfere with our listening remains within the scope of our responsibility; and in this sense here we better begin with ourselves.

Let us then consider an experience of my own that offers a reflection of my frame of mind in the course of a session in the early 1970s. (The case of Jacques is presented in Chapter 3. Here I shall only recall what is necessary to follow my reasoning.) While noting the convergence with the problems mentioned by Britton, I shall now turn to the topic I want to consider, the resistances put up to hearing and interpreting what the patient is saying. I shall begin by exploring my difficulties in putting into words an interpretation conveying what I had heard.

In the fourth year of his analysis, having in part overcome the inhibition that initially blocked his work as a writer, Jacques was repeatedly prey to severe crises of anxiety. This undermined his progress and his work. The session began with the patient recalling once more a scene from his childhood concerning his erotic curiosity about his mother's body. In previous occasions, the memory had always resisted any association, but this time the scene was associated with a dream:

I had a dream last night, of an extraordinary lunar landscape. Time had stopped. I was filled with a feeling of strangeness. From a kind of cave, there emerged a person – that person was me yet again it was not me. I looked at him, this very weird man, who was made up of a number of fragments which seemed to have been sewn together. The surrounding were those of a lunar landscape, which were familiar to me, yet unfamiliar. Strange, but already known.

You know, it makes me think now of a Russian landscape – which I know nothing about, never having been to Russia – but my father and my grandfather must have been familiar with it, both of them being Russian. [Here, Jacques falls silent for a time.]

My father was the youngest child in a large, very poor Jewish family. My grandfather had decided right from my father's birth that he would be a labourer. Only the eldest son was entitled to study. You know, in Russia, the Jews were really poor, and didn't have many opportunities. [Silence once again.]

You know, it's only right now that I realize that the thing I've always reproached my father for, when I tell you he was going to swallow me . . . I don't mean he's going to swallow me . . . what I reproach him for . . . is that he's just a worker – that he is *nothing more* – that he never tried to become somebody, to raise himself up.

Although the material that Jacques presented was new and quite amazing for both of us I could not find a way of formulating an interpretation of the transference. At the same time, I wanted to acknowledge that I had heard something new in the session. *I am dealing with my intrapsychic conflict that becomes an obstacle to interpreting.*

Some sessions later, I realized who I was in the transference. That was later. Now I notice too that in the publication I presented this material under the title: 'Surprise *in the transference*'. At this point, in the *après-coup*, I say to myself that I might very well have been closing my analytic ear so as not to listen to material from this and from many other patients that could trigger *comparable resistances.*

I (approximately) said:

You feel like a man who has been made up of different pieces originating from different places and times – a man who has been born to a situation that is old and new at the same time. As you feel that these fragments are not compatible with one another, you also feel that they require incompatible solutions. One fragment speaks to us about your father, who is also the younger-brother-condemned-not-to-study-by-his-own-father, and who therefore also condemns you in your mind, not to make progress in the pursuits that are so dear to you.

Thus did I formulate my interpretation and in so doing *overcame a strong resistance.* Reflecting on this issue I decided to take a fresh look at a text we all know well to see what could be said of my experience in this particular session. I would like now to share with my readers some thoughts prompted by my next step.

I wondered if I could find a clue by reading, from a fresh perspective, an article that, after being source of inspiration during the years of my training, remained as a symbolic link to my dearest and most respected teachers. I am speaking of Strachey's text on the mutative interpretation (1934), a classic in the sense that I shall define later. Once again, I was impressed by its rigorous construction. Strachey addresses a new idea that in 1934 needed to be backed by arguments. As the article is so well known, I only revisit it to clarify my own resistances to interpreting the new material I was hearing and to identifying the terms of my conflict. Trying to recreate the context in which the article was written I asked myself, 'To whom is he addressing this new idea?'

Strachey first states that a complete interpretation comprises two phases; in the first, the analyst functions as auxiliary superego, in the second phase, the transference is interpreted.

In a footnote, Strachey reverses the formula. Inasmuch as the id impulses must have the analyst as their object, 'the first criterion of a mutative interpretation would be that it must be a transference interpretation':

> The [. . .] original super-ego is [. . .] a product of the introjection of his archaic objects distorted by the projection of his infantile id-impulses [. . .] [I]t follows that the id-impulses – addressed by the mutative interpretations – must have the analyst as their object. If this is so, the views expressed in the present paper will require some amendment. For in that case, the first criterion of a mutative interpretation would be that it must be a transference interpretation.
>
> (op.cit.: 156)

Footnotes are an excellent means of putting forward as yet tentative thoughts. My question as to whom Strachey is addressing might perhaps receive the following answer: To analysts who do not yet favour the transference interpretation.

At this point I am able to put into words the source of my distress: *Not being able to interpret the transference and wanting to interpret the new opening I found, I felt in conflict with my psychoanalytical ideal so well stated by Strachey in that footnote. The footnote was the passage I remembered best.* Has Strachey something particular to say about my difficulty in the session? I look at what he has to say about interpretations that do not relate explicitly to the transference.

After giving extra-transference interpretations he cautions the reader:

> [T]o be specially on the *qui-vive* for transference complications. [. . .] [the extra-transference interpretations] can be made to act as 'feeders' for the transference situation, and so to *pave the way* for mutative interpretations.
>
> (op.cit.: 157 (emphasis added))

I shall quote in full the next paragraph, as this is central to what I am trying to say:

> It must not be supposed that because I am attributing these special qualities to transference interpretations, I am therefore maintaining that no others should be made. On the contrary, it is probable that a large majority of our interpretations are outside the transference – though it should be added that it often happens that when one is ostensibly giving an extra-transference interpretation one is implicitly giving a transference one. A cake cannot be made of nothing but currants; and, though it is true that extra-transference interpretations are not for the *most part* mutative, and do not themselves bring about the crucial results that involve a permanent change in the patient's mind, they are none the less essential.
>
> (op.cit.: 158 (emphasis added))

To return to the session I am presenting. At that point in the transferential history with my patient I was unable to find an interpretation of the transference. However, in my rediscovered Strachey *I find no reason for my leaving the new material aside as if it had no importance.*

In the après-coup, I wonder how frequently I might not have listened to something in the patient's discourse that might have shaken my expectations – clinical, theoretical and in a certain way as a member of a group. By leaving aside parts of Strachey's text I was taking it out of context and disrupting its fine dialectics.

Strachey also points out that the patient may tend to blur the difference between the (analyst as) auxiliary superego and his archaic superego:

> And even when the content of the auxiliary super-ego's advice is realised as being different from or contrary to that of the original super-ego, very often its quality will be felt as being the same.
>
> (op.cit.: 141)

And then, surprisingly (to me, at least), he says the following:

> [. . .] the patient may feel that the analyst has said to him, 'If you don't say whatever comes into your head, I shall give you a good hiding', or, 'If you don't become conscious of this piece of the unconscious I shall turn you out of the room.'
>
> (ibid.)

Strachey recommends that the analyst interpret the way in which the patient has listened to the interpretation. And I am astonished to find that the concept coined by me under the name of 'listening to listening' bears this antecedent that I had totally forgotten.

> Nevertheless, labile though it is, and limited as is its authority, this peculiar relation between the analyst and the patient's ego seems to put into the analyst's grasp his main instrument in assisting the development of the therapeutic process. What is this main weapon in the analyst's armoury? Its name springs at once to our lips. The weapon is, of course, interpretation.
>
> (ibid.)

I thus discover that, already in 1934, Strachey had written that the superego may carry what I would call a polyphony of texts. On my side, my attention to hearing a polyphony of texts put me in the position of recognizing the building of the superego as a condensation of three generations. (Not as if I was actually hearing the formation of the superego: I mean that my present listening allows me to render explicit the incompatible texts.)

Let us remember that in the interpretation I mentioned the incompatible pieces the patient felt he was composed of: All these elements – my forgetting of the incompatible injunctions of the archaic and the auxiliary superego, my later coining of the concept of 'listening to listening' without any reference to Strachey, the fragmentation of a text to the detriment of its rich dialectics – appear to me as different forms of narcissistic resistance, perhaps the vestiges of a *theoretical conflict*.

At this point, and only as a process of retroactive meaning, in the *après-coup*, I ask myself how often did I, for narcissistic reasons, hold back from listening to my patient's discourse? This is a question that only can be asked once this kind of resistance has been partially overcome. On the basis of this personal experience (and thinking of many other examples), I am also attempting to differentiate between a classic text and a reified text that can function as an idol at the service of *narcissistic resistances*.

How can I draw a general conclusion from this personal experience? Perhaps with reference to Italo Calvino's impressive definition of a classic as *a work that in each reading and for each reader produces new meaning*.

I had no doubt that Strachey's text was a classic. But now I can suggest a *method* that, according to Calvino, offers us a clue to recognizing a classic. Within the area of my reflection, Strachey's text has come to bear new meaning after having suffered from idealized reading, partial memory and mutilation of its dialectics. The narcissistic discourse imposed by an idol is not a classic text in the sense I have just defined.

I want to propose *that our classic texts be submitted to the test of idolatry*. If with the aim of protecting our narcissistic coherence we use them as idols – thus putting obstacles in the way of listening to our patients – if *even then* the text in a fresh reading allows each reader to find *new* meanings, we may say, once again, this is a classic.

—————— 10 ——————

APRÈS-COUP: REVISITING
WHAT HAS BEEN READ*

When writing on the concept of *après-coup* and when reflecting about this book retroactively, *après-coup*, I realized that I should avoid any temptation to propose a synthesis or anything that could be taken for a unified conception of psychoanalytical thinking. I shall seek to convey how I understand the concept and how I have been thinking psychoanalytically when using it in this book.

Après-coup is the French translation of a concept designated by Freud as *Nachträglichkeit* (noun) and *nachträglich* (adjective). The latter is a common word in German, perhaps one of the reasons why the concept of *nachträglich* and *Nachträglichkeit*, in the sense we understand *après-coup*, has not acquired in the German psychoanalytical culture the same pregnancy as it has in the French one, since translation has called for reflection.

As we know, there is no article written by Freud specifically centred on this concept. This may at least partially explain its variable fate. So we give credit to Lacan for being the first in 1953 to underline the importance of this Freudian concept referring exclusively to the *Wolf Man* case. Laplanche and Pontalis were the first to draw attention to the general importance of the concept, first in 'Fantasy and the origins of sexuality' (Laplanche and Pontalis 1964, 'Primal fantasy, fantasies of origins, origins of fantasy') and then in *The Language of Psychoanalysis* (1967). In the first article they refer to the classic paper by Susan Isaacs (1948) on unconscious *phantasy*;[1] in a perspective different from the 'principle of genetic continuity', as outlined by Isaacs, they introduce the 'operation of *après-coup*' to reflect on (among other problems) the status of fantasy.

Nachträglichkeit was translated by Strachey as 'deferred action'. As Laplanche points out, in certain contexts in Freud's work this translation is correct. By

* Part of this chapter is based on a paper presented in 1998 at the Standing Conference on Psychoanalytical Intracultural and Intercultural Dialogue, 26 July 1998.

choosing this term, Strachey was trying to convey the idea of a link between two moments. But the word 'deferred' suggests also a linear conception of time. It also expresses a direction of the arrow of time in a sense opposite to that suggested by *après-coup*, which is *retroactivity*.[2] The choice of translation involves perhaps a particular way of conceiving temporalization and psychic causality.

Revisiting the concept of *après-coup* in Freud's work would involve revisiting all his work, insofar as this notion is linked to the theory of seduction, trauma, biphasic sexual development, etc. As far as I am concerned, I shall only make a brief comment in relation to adolescence and to construction. As to the latter, I think that the concept of *après-coup* can be integrated into the Freudian definition of construction (1919a, 1937) as we saw in Chapter 3.

In relation to adolescence, I am resorting to my clinical experience in the course of analysing adult patients. Privileged moments have arisen – as I remarked it has been the case in every advanced analysis in my practice – in which there is a fragmentary *reconstruction of historical truths relating to the adolescence of the analysands*. The analysis enables the patient to put into words the way in which, in passing through adolescence, he found himself faced with new constraints that produce a demand for psychic work and hence with different types of conflict. This reconstruction, which, I insist, occurs in a fragmentary way, takes place at different moments in the analytical process, in particular on the occasion of the significant resumption of a conflict in the history of the transference. The Freudian idea of a sexuality that develops in two stages and the operation of *après-coup* give theoretico–clinical support to this clinical discovery (Faimberg 1998b).

In France, the need to theorize about *après-coup* arises first and foremost in the dialogue with other psychoanalytical cultures, which explains why the French literature devoted to this topic is less abundant than one might have expected.[3] Even so, revisiting the literature on the topic would mean revisiting the history of psychoanalytical thinking, particularly in France. So I am considering *one* of the possible ways of thinking about the problem from a personal and more limited perspective.

As I said in Chapter 7, from a strictly Freudian point of view the concept of *Nachträglichkeit* could be defined exclusively as 'the assignment of new meaning to memory traces'. In Chapters 1, 2 and 3, in which I explicitly referred to *historicization and après-coup*, I have discovered, retroactively, that I had used (at the time when they were written) the concept of *après-coup* in a much broader sense than Freud. This was due, as the reader may have realized, to my clinical experience in which I was led to explore the *narcissistic links between generations*.

This extension of the concept allowed me to give new meanings (and even simply for the first time *a* meaning) to the analysand's *narcissistic way* of functioning. It also allowed me to understand how the analysand may *modify his position as a subject* in relation to something that psychically took place in early infancy, even before speech. I should like the reader to join me in thinking about this extension of the concept and thus to give fresh thought to the concept of *Nachträglichkeit*.

I consider that the operation of *après-coup* consists in *two inseparable* phases, one of *anticipation* and another of *retrospection*. This twofold movement is always present when I speak of *après-coup*. This is my option, mainly presented in chapters on (re)construction (Chapter 3), on 'Listening to listening and *après-coup*' (Chapter 7) and on 'Misunderstanding and psychic truths' (Chapter 8). The Freudian concept of 'complementary series' helps to understand that this movement is complex and related in reciprocal causation, i.e. dialectical.[4] Therefore there is a non-linear, dialectical conception of time in the concept of *après-coup*.

From what point in time does the après-coup operation come into effect in the psychoanalytical process? I realized that in each chapter I considered the operation of *après-coup* as taking place in the present time of the analytical session and giving retroactive significance to a previous experience. Moreover, the two points in time are linked by a relationship of meaning. For this latter reason the operation of *après-coup* is different from a *fantasy* of *après-coup* (as accurately pointed out by Laplanche and Pontalis (1967) and Neyraut (1997)). Indeed, Jung thought that retroactive fantasizing (*Zurückphantasieren*) shaped the past, which led him to reject Freud's central theory of infantile sexuality.

Paradoxical as it might seem, I shall quote an example from an author who never used (at least explicitly) the concept of *après-coup*. Yet it is in my view a splendid illustration of the *extended concept of après-coup I proposed*. I am referring to Winnicott's 'Fear of breakdown' (1974). (Although, as I said, I presented this idea for the first time at the aforementioned conference in 1998, I realized retroactively that this was in a certain way already foreshadowed in 1981 in Chapter 2.)

As we know, Winnicott interprets that the breakdown, which the patient fears will inexorably occur in the future, already took place at a time when there was, properly speaking, no subject to experience it. What happens in the present (fear of breakdown) is linked to what has already occurred (a primitive agony) *by a relationship of meaning*. And this relationship is established *as an operation of après-coup, by way of a construction*. I consider this process as an operation of *après-coup* in the larger sense I am proposing and *not* in the sense given by Freud in his letter to Fliess (1896).[5]

This means linking the broader concept of *après-coup* to a particular way of conceptualizing the process of (re)construction as already mentioned in Chapter 3. It allows us to consider a kind of construction as having a status similar to that given, precisely by Freud (1919), to the second phase of the girl's fantasy in 'A child is being beaten'.[6]

We said in the aforementioned chapter that in some cases there is nothing to remember: Only repetition allows us to grasp 'a piece of the early history that the patient has forgotten' (Freud 1937) and to propose a construction that provides a new and unprecedented link in the *après-coup*. By this link, the past is constituted as such and the patient acquires a history. Now we can add that Winnicott provides a new link by which the primitive agony is constituted as *past*.

'A piece of the early history that the patient has forgotten', as Freud writes of construction, may be equivalent to the 'disaster that already took place when there was not a subject to experience it', mentioned by Winnicott. In this joint approach to *après-coup* and construction (with the construction of the patient's past), the dilemma often posed, between interpreting in the present or interpreting in the past, would appear in a new light.

Already in 1936 Joan Rivière, writing about the negative therapeutic reaction, stated:

> [. . .] *the worst disasters have actually taken place*; it is this truth that [the patient] will not allow the analysis to make real, will not allow to be 'realized' by him or us.
>
> (Rivière 1936: 312 (emphasis added))

Something that has already taken place in the psyche and is projected into the future[7] is basically a Freudian standpoint.[8] While Winnicott stresses the *Hilflosigkeit* (in this case, primitive agony), Joan Rivière theoretically articulates her remarks with Melanie Klein's depressive position. In my perspective one of the most outstanding characteristics of Klein's theory of the depressive position concerns the inclusion of a particular dimension of time, as mentioned in Chapter 2. The movement of *après-coup* as such, although not formulated, appears even more evident to my mind in Winnicott's paper than in that of Rivière.

Historicization and *après-coup*

It is not uncommon to regard as history the material events in the past. In France, Serge Viderman (1970) has critically discussed this approach. From our viewpoint, expressed in Chapters 3 and 8, we consider that material events in the past *as such* are never to be considered as history (in its *psychoanalytical* relevance). The way material events, intrapsychic historical truths, unconscious psychic reality and solipsism may be articulated has been in particular developed in Chapter 8.

What is of interest from the psychoanalytical viewpoint is the way in which material events ask for *psychic work*. We have seen from different perspectives how this psychic work has been recognized in the psychoanalytical process: In the case of Jacques (Chapters 3 and 9) through a dream and his associations; in

Mario's case (Chapter 1) especially through the anachronism of 'the "two pesos" dollars' (discovered through the 'enigma posed by the transference'). (For this concept, see also Faimberg (1992).)

As I said in my introduction, I limit the reworking of the original articles to stylistic revision and the suppression of repetitive material. *Après-coup*, I think that in Chapter 1, I did not sufficiently stress Mario's unconscious desire, his psychic activity, in the forming of unconscious identifications. The reason is that I was so impressed by the discovery of the alienating aspect, of my analysand's subjugation to the previous generation(s), that I dwelt on the passive split-off.

To illustrate the difference I establish between information and story, on one side, and *history*, on the other, I should like to recall a sequence in the clinical material presented in Chapter 8. In her adolescence, Brigitte had received information about her filiation. The 'material event' in itself (the non-biological father) does not deserve, from my point of view, to be called 'history'. Also, according to my chosen option, the 'mother's discourse' should be called 'story' and not 'history'. It is only at this point that Brigitte recognizes the still unconscious *active effects* of the 'story' by bringing it in her associations during the session. This will enable her to transform it into 'history'.

To understand this better, let us remember the following sequence:

Analyst: Through my interpretation, it is possible that we – you and I – are hearing someone who treats you as if you were worthless. If so . . ., I wonder who it might be?

My 'listening to listening' function and my reinterpretation followed by her associations led us to an *intrapsychic unconscious scene*. At this point, retroactively, this scene serves to provide an unconscious context to my first interpretation (the one I felt was not adequate). This intrapsychic unconscious scene is characterized by the discourse of a mother who deprives her daughter of a father through her contempt and lack of concern. From the perspective that I am proposing, this unconscious scene allows a meaning to be given *après-coup* to my interpretation beyond what I thought I had said.

From then on, because we had access to the intrapsychic unconscious scene, there is an opening and the conditions are given for my interpreting:

By telling me about your efforts to get pregnant, perhaps you were trying to explore what are you entitled to, what is a legitimate desire and who confers legitimacy.

Brigitte then says: 'My father saved my life and he's my real dad.'

In this sequence, I was interested in following some of the complex and reciprocal resignifications that transform the psychic effectiveness of the mother's discourse. We can say that the 'listening to listening' function and my reinterpretations, through the operation of *après-coup*, resignify the past: There, where the mother's discourse had the intrapsychic effect of depriving her of a father, the sequence in the session leads her to have access to an intrapsychic 'dad', i.e. access to a father, to an intrapsychic triangulation.

Après-coup is operating both in the analysis of misunderstanding and in the way that this story (as associated) receives a new meaning. At this moment, the story is transformed into *her history*. And reciprocally this resignification gives new meaning to her attempt to become pregnant with a fatherless child.

I pointed before to the dilemma that is frequently posed as to whether we should interpret in the present or in the past. Moreover, it is worth recalling here the widely made assertion that when the patient (or the analyst in some cases) prefers interpretations in the past (*alibi et tunc*) he is showing a resistance to the 'here and now' (*hic et nunc*). And I would add that the converse may also be true. But this is not the problem that I wish to probe since in both cases *the dilemma remains*.

The fact is that, in the operation of *après-coup*, a complex and reciprocal temporal dialectic comes into play, a dialectical logic that establishes the possible conditions for overcoming the dilemma. (The dilemma, on the contrary, relies on a *binary* logic: The alternative of '*either/or*'.)

The unconscious scene in the case of Brigitte – a scene which I consider to be of key importance – belongs *simultaneously* to the present and to all possible meaningful pasts, *constituted as such by the operation of après-coup*.

I would like to put forward the following conclusion. The operation of *après-coup* contributes to solving the dilemma as to whether we should interpret in the present or in the past. The past is constituted as such by the operation of *après-coup*.

The same passage from story to history appears in the cases of Mario and Jacques. Let us just underline that once the process of disalienation (or disidentification) with the father's history has taken place, Mario is able to find the appropriate questions to put to his mother and receive adequate answers. I mean by this that there is a process of disidentification to an alienated unconscious narcissistic identification, therefore a process of disalienation.

Mario then brings to analysis the secret story of his Aunt Rita. The operation of *après-coup* even allows Mario, so to speak, to 'construct a memory': 'I realized that Aunt Rita existed.' This 'creation' of a memory is the consequence of the disidentification to the disavowal which both parents mantained toward their own histories. By bringing the secret of her existence to the transference Mario is able to articulate the way Aunt Rita's story concerned *him* and thus transform it into *his history*. We could also reconstruct the possible infantile psychotic episode when the patient's brother was born and Mario 'stopped playing, stopped talking'.

So, when we consider the psychoanalytical process in itself, it can be said that, in the history of the transference, as we listen to the unconscious, conflicts can be resignified, screen memories (Freud 1899) can be decondensated and indeed even memories can be created. From the standpoint I have presented, we can say that this is an instance of the operation of *après-coup*. Finally, let us note that the operation of *après-coup* is always understood in articulation with other psychoanalytical concepts that need to be contextualized in the way of thinking and working of a particular analyst, tradition or school.

Let my conclusion be not a closing but an opening. The question is *how* do analysts belonging to other traditions deal with the clinical and theoretical problems that *I would formulate in terms of après-coup*? Can it be said that their approach to these problems points to an *absent concept*? Or do they tackle these problems from another perspective?

Those analysts who propose another perspective no doubt consider that *après-coup* cannot be regarded as an absent concept in their work. But even if this is so, *does the concept of après-coup open up new avenues in psychoanalytical theory and clinical experience*? I have sought possible answers to this question by addressing the process of *après-coup* from different perspectives in each chapter in this book.

As we have seen, links between generations are conceived in this book from a strictly psychoanalytical point of view and take into account the presence of an 'other' who participates from the beginning with his own psyche, including his unconscious psyche, in the constitution of the subject's psychic makeup. All this implies a process that permits the recognition (in the history of the transference) of the conflictual modalities that place a human being in relationship with the generations that preceded his or her birth.

We observe in different clinical cases how we may discover (with surprise where neither the patient nor the analyst expects it) what may be called the 'third object of the other':[9] In the case of Alice, this 'third object' is 'Alice's narcissistic grandmother', which is the 'maternal object of Alice's mother' as inscribed in the *patient's unconscious psychic* reality (Chapter 5). In the case of Mario, the 'third object' is Mario's father's Polish family and his mother's sister Rita, as inscribed in the patient's unconscious psychic reality (Chapter 1). In the case of Jacques, this 'third object' is his paternal Russian grandfather and his mother's brother, the writer, as inscribed in the patient's unconscious psychic reality (Chapter 3). In the particular case of Jacques, the 'third object' is discovered through his associations to a dream; this allowed me to understand that the 'third object of the other' may be found in every advanced analysis. This initial intuition was confirmed in my own cases and in those cases I have supervised over a long period of time.

We also consider in which way the history preceding the conception of the subject may be (re)constructed *après-coup* in the psychoanalytical process. This is paradigmatically evident in the case of Mario. What this case taught me became the original cause for my interest in what I have named since then the 'telescoping of generations' and in the 'narcissistic links between generations'.

I wondered in Chapter 1 if this process of transmission between generations may not be a universal phenomenon to be discovered in every analysis. Here again this initial intuition was confirmed through my clinical experience.[10]

The linking process between generations mediated by certain unconscious identifications revealed in the same process of (re)construction. As I said, insofar as these identifications partly depend on the story that belongs to another generation, such identifications are alienating. Their cause lies in the history of an 'other'. I have referred to this form of identification as 'unconscious alienated narcissistic identification'. Here, as elsewhere, 'cause' is always used in the sense of 'condition of possibility' and not as a 'term-to-term' relation.

Considering therefore that my chosen perspective implies that *unconscious alienated identifications have a history*, in my interpretative activity I listen to the interplay of interpretation/reinterpretation in order to emphasize the historical context and thereby discover '*who* is speaking'.

This conceptualization of the relationship between generations is not aimed at ascertaining whether it is necessary to go further and further back in chronological time,[11] which is made clear in 'The Oedipus myth revisited' (Chapter 6). It is geared to what is at issue in the transference, i.e. listening to the anachronisms of the unconscious (which is particularly eloquent in Mario's case) and to the (re)construction of intrapsychical historical truths (as in the cases of Lise (Chapter 2) and Brigitte (Chapter 8)). The notion of 'intergenerational relationship', or 'links between generations', should not be used to anticipate, on the basis of known events, what might be brought to light only by the analytical process.

Now is the time for me, *après-coup*, to make certain acknowledgements. In Chapter 1, I wrote that 'Freud examines the different moments that enable the subject to differentiate himself from the object. According to the logic of narcissism, regulated by the principle of pleasure–unpleasure, the following equation is proposed. The ego is the equivalent of pleasure and the non-ego is the equivalent of unpleasure.' Here I wish to add that Bion (1962a, 1962b), Marion Milner (1952) and Winnicott (1953, 1960a) have addressed this issue from different perspectives.

At the time that Antoine Corel and I wrote our essay on construction we were not aware that Theodor Reik was the first analyst to write about surprise in psychoanalysis, in a book published in 1935. For this reason he was not quoted in our essay. Following my method of only introducing minor modifications to the original texts, I am including his name in the general bibliography. Re-reading Heinrich Racker's papers on countertransference I found that he occasionally uses, from his particular perspective, the term of 'countertransference position', a term that I propose in Chapter 4 as a neologism.

In Chapter 8, I say: 'It is not for the analyst to impose an adaptation to his own implicit or explicit criteria about reality; these may be very unreal to the patient when he is living in a different psychic reality.' Having read the work of Hans Loewald after having written the essays that compose this book, I find, *après-coup*, that here I am in the same position as this author in his article 'Ego and reality' (1951). I have also found deep coincidences with Loewald on many other points, but this deserves a study in itself.

In almost every chapter, I have stressed the importance of the concept of disavowal (*Verleugnung*).[12] The Freudian concept of *Verleugnung* should be carefully distinguished from the Freudian concepts of *Verdrängung* (repression) and *Verneinung* (negation).[13]

Finally, as already mentioned in my introduction, this book outlines a journey, which I imagined as my quest for the 'Snark'. This is why I wish to conclude this book with my essay on Lewis Carroll's poem, *The Hunting of the Snark*.

'THE SNARK WAS A BOOJUM';* READING LEWIS CARROLL (1977)

'For the Snark *was* a Boojum, you see.' Thus concludes Lewis Carroll's poem, *The Hunting of the Snark* (1876). With this statement he started writing his 'agony', as he called it. Carroll himself (quoted by Gardner 1967) said the phrase imposed itself on him:[1] The words had preceded him without his knowing what they meant, either at that moment or when he wrote the poem as a whole. He accepted interpretations ironically. I expect the one I am offering him will preserve the poetical beauty of its riddle and that, in a certain sense, what is revealed will leave the hidden untouched. Carroll turned the statement into an evidence of being: 'Was . . . you see.' For that reason I thought it right to use the last line of the poem as a title.

'The Snark *was* a Boojum.' Two subjects are correlated in their existence. *Two neologisms signify each other: A pure open significance.* In their correlation an interstice was left that called for a development. And Carroll developed it as a 'tragedy'. There is a prophecy and an inexorable fulfilment. The one stating it inscribes another one, as we shall see, in a predetermined and fatal structure that starts by sharing the same name, a forgotten name that never appears.

> '"But oh, beamish nephew, beware of the day,
> If your Snark be a Boojum! For then
> You will softly and suddenly vanish away,
> And never be met with again!"'

('Fit the Third')

---

* First published in the *International Review of Psychoanalysis*.

Analysis of the poem

The preface

Carroll assures us that it is 'wildly possible' that the author of 'this brief but instructive poem' may be accused of writing 'nonsense'. He could ground his defence on the facts that in the story one can find both strong moral purposes and teachings on arithmetic and natural history as well. He is convinced that the accusation will be caused by this line: 'Then the bowsprit got mixed with the rudder sometimes' ('Fit the Second').

His defence, he says, will merely consist in explaining how things happened. We are surprised to find that he does not provide a lineal explanation based on an anecdote, as he seems to anticipate. Instead, he presents *a rule* ('rule 42'), postulating: 'No one shall speak to the Man of the Helm', which the Bellman, chief of the Snark-hunting expedition, completes with a reciprocal rule: 'And the Man of the Helm shall speak to no one'.

The 'nonsense' acquires sense when it is understood that there had been another story with other rules explaining what would be inexplicable if it were understood at a single level. *This rule narcissistically regulates the interruption of any reciprocal discourse, thus creating the necessary conditions for 'Snarkization' to take place.*

Once the narcissistic structure is ruled, the nonsense is organized. Obviously, Carroll is to blame: He is guilty of having discovered *other rules in another scene*. That is why he speaks about the lay of the Jabberwock pointing out that *there is a law for nonsense*, that it is *not lacking in legality*, only it is *a different kind of legality* from the one we know.

He gives us an exhilarating lesson in phonetics on 'human perversity' in tergiversating the pronunciation, the scandal of neologism creation being neglected in this decentralization. Once the existence of other rules is put forth categorically, he tells us about Humpty Dumpty's theory of the multiple sense of words: 'Humpty Dumpty's theory *of two meanings packed into one word like a portmanteau, seems to me the right explanation for all.*' And he encourages us to overcome our misgivings by telling the story of one such word: 'Rilchiam'. It is the right symmetry for Père Ubu's *merdre*.

'Fit the First: The Landing'

'Just the place for a Snark!', the Bellman cried.

Snark is a portmanteau word. Remember Humpty Dumpty's law! The Oxford English Dictionary defines 'portmanteau word' as a fictitious word that blends the sounds and combines the meanings of two others (e.g. slithy = lithe and slimy). According to Carroll (quoted by Gardner) Snark is a 'packing' of snail and shark. (Greenacre, quoted by the same source, adds snake.) In my opinion, with a shade supporting my point of view, snarl could be added. The OED gives 'snarl': '(of dog) make high-pitched quarrelsome growl; (of person) speak cynically, make ill-tempered complaints or criticisms – snarl out – utter in.' With all this, something of the order of the word should be condensed. *Thus the multiple significance of the word would be poeticized and scientifically explained by the law of Humpty Dumpty*:

'Just the place for a Snark! I have said it twice:
That alone should encourage the crew.
Just the place for a Snark! I have said it thrice:
What I tell you three times is true.'

The memorable rule of three is first formulated here. What you say three times *is* true. The possibility of change and reasoning is thus mockingly suppressed as a function of repetition. The repetition–compulsion states as truth phrases that impose themselves, insisting significants. The Bellman is chief of the crew that is about to sail. He states the *place*. He will state the *time*. Comments such as 'We have hardly a minute to waste', 'Any further delay and we shan't catch a Snark before night', 'Skip all that!' provide the temporal dimension. Gardner comments that on early ships the Bellman was the one announcing the time by striking a bell at eight different times and connects this with the eight 'fits' the poem is composed of.

The Bellman is the one who announces the rule of three; the one who acknowledges the method for catching the Snark; the one announcing schizo-phrenicizing rules. He gives speeches to cheer up the crew. His only guiding gesture for crossing the sea is striking a bell. He provides truth criteria. He marks the position, makes decisive statements, points out landmarks: He is, in effect, the chorus.

As regards the composition of the 10 members of the crew, F. C. S. Schiller in 'Snarkophilus Snobbs' (quoted by Gardner op. cit.: 106) makes a remark that should be taken into account. When remarking that the name of every member of the crew starts with 'B' (and, as Gardner says in reference to *Alice in Wonderland's* March Hare who, in an analogous situation, answers 'Why not?') he says that this repetition of 'B' must mean: 'To be or not to be?' A statement is thus advanced in connection with *whether a subject is or is not, at a given place, through a period of time, for a Snark*.

The 10 members of the crew have different professions. Apart from the Bellman (the chief), there is the Beaver, a potential victim of the Butcher, who makes lace and can save people from the wreck, although no one knows how. The Butcher can only kill beavers. As there is just one animal aboard, the Bellman says its life must be protected. The Banker, 'engaged at enormous expense', is in charge of all the cash on board, fails to endorse cheques before a monster and offers a policy to protect the Beaver's life against fire and damage from hail. The

Baker, the hero of this tragedy, can only make Bridecake, the ingredients for which are unavailable. Unlike the other members of the crew, he is not called after his profession; it is just mentioned that he has *forgotten his name* and carries out *the function* of a baker. Having 'a small intellect' and 'a perfect courage', he makes jokes to hyenas and takes walks with a bear 'just to keep up its spirit'. That is, *he does it for nothing, a condition making possible an extraordinary adventure*. The Baker forgot his name when forgetting the 42 packages; he forgot to say he had forgotten them. He is the one who shall suffer the prophecy and the one who will be unable to free himself of it, because he forgot it was in English that they were speaking. Thus he makes an allusion to something in connection with memory. It is remarkable how the whole of the crew has impossible professions.

'Fit the Second: The Bellman's Speech'

The Bellman, a wise man, brought a map that could be understood by everyone: It only represented the sea, with no lands; a blank map. He would not use Mercator's because:

'They are merely conventional signs!

[. . .] (So the crew would protest) that he's bought *us* the best –
A perfect and absolute blank!'

The OED gives a double and antithetical meaning to the word 'protest'. On the one hand, it means 'disapprove'. On the other, it means 'affirming something solemnly'. It is in both senses that the 'protest' of the crew must be considered, because this absolute blank makes it possible to share something in a perfect way, but precisely at the cost of *abolishing the conventional signs constituting the language* (see also Donnet and Green 1973).

Having lost the possibility of communicating with one another through language (remember that now comes the passage referred to by Carroll in the Preface, where rule 42 of non-communication with the Man of the Helm is specified) the Captain, whom they trusted, loses every notion of how to cross the ocean, except a magic gesture, striking a bell:

When he cried, 'Steer to starboard, but keep her head larboard!'
What on earth was the helmsman to do?

Then the bowsprit got mixed with the rudder sometimes:
A thing, as the Bellman remarked,
That frequently happens in tropical climes,
When a vessel is, so to speak, 'snarked'.

The Bellman gives the most contradictory orders, which co-exist without any discrimination. The snarkization is produced where the different parts of the ship body are all mixed up and confused: Displacement and condensation are the laws giving sense to 'nonsense': Humpty Dumpty's law full enacted. Gardner speaks about a science fiction story where there is a *'snarkized'* city. It means that *nothing can be accepted that has not been repeated three times.* Repetition–compulsion: Full prevalence of death compulsion.

Space is dislocated:

[. . .] when the wind blew due East,
[. . .] the ship would [. . .] travel due West.

After this moment of insanity and depression, musical tones and inarticulate disapproving sounds are mentioned. It is not possible to re-establish language yet. There is a toast. The Bellman says:

'Friends, Romans, and countrymen, lend me your ears!'
(They were all of them fond of quotations:
So they drank to his health, and they gave him three cheers,
While he served out additional rations.)

A shared speech unites them. Culture. England. Shakespeare. A tautological, self-sufficient time is an ironical attempt at a formalization of insanity:

'We have sailed many months, we have sailed many weeks,
(Four weeks to the month you may mark),
But never as yet ('tis your captain who speaks)
Have we caught the least glimpse of a Snark!'

The Snark is given a visual and fugitive character (glimpse). His five characteristics are beginning to be outlined. '*Hollow*' refers both to emptiness, a hole, that which is not solid and to what is false and insincere. The first characteristic of the Snark is: Something that goes in through the mouth, *hole-like, like an absence.* But it also has a *consistency* ('crisp'). Therefore, it is an *absence that is present, with a consistency like a non-object with a psychic reality of presence* (Faimberg 1976).

'Its habit of getting up late you'll agree
That it carries too far, when I say
That it frequently breakfasts at five-o'clock tea,
And dines on the following day.'

A time that displaces itself: The time of the unconscious. Let us think of the famous eternal tea party of *Alice in Wonderland*:

'The third is its slowness in taking a jest.
Should you happen to venture on one,
It will sigh like a thing that is deeply distressed:
And it always looks grave at a pun.'

(emphasis added)

Neither the joke nor the pun appears as its characteristics: It lacks a symbolic dimension. Its fourth quality is 'fondness for bathing-machines'. A reference, I suppose, to Victorian customs, the hypocrisy of hiding the body, a whole grotesque-poetical allusion giving rise to beauty in this context. And it is also ambitious, ambitious to become a Boojum, I suspect:

'Some are Boojums . . .' The Bellman broke off in alarm,
For the Baker had fainted away.

My suspicion is confirmed: Being a Boojum *is* its ambition. Now the tragedy can be seen. There is a failure in consciousness. This demands an explanation. The next Fit will develop it.

'Fit the Third: The Baker's Tale'

They roused him with muffins – they roused him with ice –
They roused him with mustard and cress –
They roused him with jam and judicious advice –
They set him conundrums to guess.

(emphasis added)

They rouse the Baker with conundrums, invoking the multiple meaning of words. They place him before unknown things. Finally, he is able to talk and proposes to tell his story, in an 'antediluvian tone' in reference to his *archaic* past.

'My father and mother were honest, though poor – '
'Skip all that!', cried the Bellman in haste.
'If it once becomes dark, there's no chance for a Snark –
We have hardly a minute to waste!'

'I skip forty years', said the Baker, in tears,
'And proceed without further remark
To the day when you took me aboard of your ship
To help you in hunting the Snark.'

His story begins with commonplace, empty words: A trivial story. The Bellman marks the time, points out the task, urges them to hurry up. Gardner

122

mentions the repetition of the number 42. The rule 42 of the Preface, the 42 packages; Carroll wrote the poem when he was 42 years old. By skipping 40 years, the Baker has started his story at the age of two (Carroll's, of course), the time when the acquisition of language is at full swing. (I have taken the liberty of making this little reference to the author, in order to point out this curiosity.) Which is revealed by the comment: 'and he was able to speak'. When he skips the next 40 years, the story is condensed to a single situation: The day of the sailing for the hunting of the Snark:

'A dear uncle of mine (after whom I was named)
Remarked, when I bade him farewell – '
'Oh, skip your dear uncle!' the Bellman exclaimed,
As he angrily tingled his bell.

His story starts with his name, which has been forgotten, the same name of his dear uncle, which does not appear either. This places him in a past that determines his future *already* from his name. *Thus a prophecy arises: The best way of 'futurizing' a past, as a form of unconscious temporality*:

'He remarked to me then', said that mildest of men,
'"If your Snark be a Snark, that is right:
Fetch it home by all means – you may serve it with greens,
And it's handy for striking a light."'

For the first time a method for hunting Snarks is mentioned. This is a treasure of surrealistic poetry:

'"You may seek it with thimbles – and seek it with care –
You may hunt it with forks and hope;
You may threaten its life with a railway-share;
You may charm it with smiles and soap – "'

Here it may be seen how the method for hunting the Snark is a poetical and nonsensical one. Thus the Snark becomes the significant creator par excellence, being open to all meanings. Only a Snark could have used such a method:

('That's exactly the method,' the Bellman bold
In a hasty parenthesis cried,
'That's exactly the way I have always been told
That the capture of Snarks should be tried!')

The Bellman *acknowledges the object through the method*. By way of contrast, Holiday, the artist who illustrated the poem in its original edition, probes into

123

his own method of representation. When illustrating the method for the hunting, a woman appears. 'Who is this beautiful young lady?', asks Carroll. 'Hope, naturally', answers Holiday. And adds triumphantly: 'I have discovered the third meaning of "with"' (mentioned by Gardner). The artist draws as in a dream, he, who formally seemed to be too 'classical' to illustrate the poem, understood that he *had to draw a text* and not just illustrate the poem: *The drawing is the poem, too.* Something in the order of *words*, now that the *conditions of representability* have been settled by the artist himself, imposed itself on the writer. Lewis Carroll approves: A new significance has been revealed to him:

'"But oh, beamish nephew, beware of the day,
If your Snark be a Boojum! For then
You will softly and suddenly vanish away,
And never be met with again!"'

The prophecy is put forth. If it is the Snark that is being sought, the uncle has said, it is all right. Because it will be an unending and impossible search, with a crew who have impossible professions, for a fleeting and equally impossible object. The exercise of literary creation is guaranteed. But if the Snark gets into an absolute and permanent correspondence with another significant (Boojum), so that one becomes the meaning of the other, the incessant search for significances that makes it possible for this subject to live in a symbolic world shall be stopped, once and for all. *There will not be any more multiple senses, or portmanteau words. It will not be possible to say 'beamish':*

'It is this, it is this that oppresses my soul,
When I think of my uncle's last words [. . .]'

Once more the artist interprets 'last words': Those uttered on the deathbed:

'But if ever I meet with a Boojum, that day,
In a moment (of this I am sure),
I shall softly and suddenly vanish away –
And the notion I cannot endure!'

The appearance of death anguish and fainting denounces the possibility of disappearance of the subject in a radical way. It is the unbearable notion each of us has that he is going to die. Death, emptiness, the interruption of all significance. The nameless dread mentioned by Bion (1962b); the object '(a)' defined by Lacan (1965) and elaborated by Green (1973) and Leclaire (1971), the 'catastrophic anguish avoided by the phobic' (Mom 1960).

The strange fascination exercised by the Snark, even knowing the ambitious possibility that it might be a Boojum, may be felt in the following lines:

'I engage with the Snark – every night after dark –
In a dreamy delirious fight:
I serve it with greens in those shadowy scenes,
And I use it for striking a light:'

Which reveals the oneiric character of the fight.

'Fit the Fourth: The Hunting'

The Bellman looked uffish, and wrinkled his brow.
'If only you'd spoken before!
It's excessively awkward to mention it now,
With the Snark, so to speak, at the door!'

Uffish (quoted by Gardner): '*Jabberwocky. A state of mind when the voice is gruffish, the manner roughish and the temper huffish*' (op. cit.: 67). It seems to refer to a condition that is typical of anxious depression. At the door of the limit situation, the prophecy cannot *but* be fulfilled. They are embarked on a trip that the Bellman will not interrupt. The nameless one, who knows his fate, not only forgot his name, but also to communicate to the others the danger he was in. There are references that place the Bellman as the chorus, pointing out the steps of the tragedy; the language Greek is mentioned in the next stanza.

'I said it in Hebrew – I said it in Dutch –
I said it in German and Greek:
But I wholly forget (and it vexes me much)
That English is what you speak!'

(emphasis added)

He had lost intersubjectivity, language is no longer communication for him. Other languages for the transmission of knowledge appear, but the present language, their own, is lost. This knowledge was, then, *a knowledge without a subject and for no one*; with the atemporality of the unconscious:

'For the Snark's a peculiar creature, that wo'n't
Be caught in a commonplace way.'

The Snark is a privileged significant, alien to commonplace: It has already been characterized as a fugitive. *The fugitive significant of poetic creation*:

'Do all that you know, and try all that you don't:
Not a chance must be wasted to-day!'

125

The discourse following this is in accordance with the exercise of impossible tasks carried out by an impossible crew. First, a speech on patriotic duties. Then empty gestures. The Banker endorses a blank cheque, which he crosses. The Beaver makes lace, 'galumphing about' at seeing the Butcher so shy and sobbing. 'Be a man!', says the Bellman – a regressive and useless order. 'Should we meet with a Jubjub, that desperate bird . . .' Then the Butcher does not have a single idea. Terrible subrogates of the object can be anticipated. I think that another concealed phrase is evoked here. Shakespeare again: 'It was the nightingale . . .' that sets the limit to Romeo and Juliet's love night.

'Fit the Fifth: The Beaver's Lesson'

For the third time the method for hunting the Snark is repeated. Thus it is established as the right one. The Butcher and the Beaver – a potential killer and a potential victim respectively – are left alone in front of each other each conceiving the idea of the Snark, the same plan for hunting it down and suffering the same panic. The Butcher thinks of his childhood:

"'Tis the voice of the Jubjub!'" he suddenly cried.

Gardner refers here to *Alice in Wonderland*: 'Tis the voice of the Lobster.' I have already anticipated: 'It was the nightingale':

'I have uttered that sentiment once.'

'Tis the song of the Jubjub! The proof is complete,
If only I've stated it thrice.'

A nameless terror before that feeling that had been uttered before. Feeling is mediated in this way by words. *They are looking for a word that may express the nameless feeling: Jubjub.* And the *rule of three*: 'If only I've stated it thrice.' Repetition sanctions what is true. The Butcher gives the Beaver an exhilarating mathematics lesson. In this lesson, he presents a perfect tautology developed as a science. The starting point is the rule of three. Science in the service of terror and of repetition. The lesson in natural history describes the characteristics of the Jubjub, which is, I think, a subrogate of the Snark:

'As to temper the Jubjub's a desperate bird.
Since it lives in perpetual passion:'

'Snarl' also refers to canine noises. All this creates a fantastic world of animals and noises. Let us remember the subsequent occurrence of the Bandersnatch, nightingales, lobsters, bears, hyenas, pigs.

126

'Fit the Sixth: The Barrister's Dream'

The Snark can only be perceived in a dream. It is the only case in which the artist working with Carroll represented it. The Boojum conceived by Holiday was never published. *Carroll insisted that the Boojum could not be represented.* A day residue of the dream is the Beaver making lace and the Barrister declaring the illegality of that activity. The Snark carries out all the functions; he accuses and defends, he reads out the sentence. There is an impossible trial where a pig accused of abandoning the stable is condemned:

'Transportation for life', was the sentence it gave,
'And *then* to be fined forty pound.'

The punishment cannot be applied: The pig had died years before. Nonsense at the service of the logic of the unconscious: Atemporality and persecution.

'Fit the Seventh: The Banker's Fate'

The Banker faces another subrogate of the Snark: The Bandersnatch. Another hideous animal. The Banker endorses cheques, but is unable to subdue it. Another failure in his profession. Insane, he is abandoned to his fate.

Thesis on the dangers of hunting the snark

'Fit the Eighth: The Vanishing'

The method is mentioned for the sixth time. Once more the Bellman narrates the events:

'There is Thingumbob shouting!' the Bellman said,
'He is shouting like mad, only hark!
He is waving his hands, he is wagging his head,
He has certainly found a Snark!'
[. . .]
Erect and sublime, for one moment of time,
In the next, that wild figure they saw
(As if stung by a spasm) plunge into a chasm,
While they waited and listened in awe.

'It's a Snark!' was the sound that first came to their ears,
And seemed almost too good to be true.

Then followed a torrent of laughter and cheers:
Then the ominous words: 'It's a Boo – '
[. . .]
In the midst of the word he was trying to say,
In the midst of his laughter and glee,
He had softly and suddenly vanished away –
For the Snark *was* a Boojum, *you see.*[2]

The nameless hero, the victim of his uncle's prophecy, seeking his forgotten name, embarked on the poetic adventure, finds the Snark and becomes an erect figure. The Snark is no longer a significant; he is materialized in the phallic figure of the hero. The Hero *is* the Phallus. But this identification is 'too good to be true': It provokes laughter, then tears . . . then silence. Once the absolute significance has been found the subject disappears.

This is my thesis: *This poem is the retroactive construction of a poetical–prophetic end where, through the literary adventure of creation of 'nonsense', the disappearance of the subject is effected through the absolute encounter of two significants: Snark–Boojum. Either of them becomes the meaning on the other one and thus the incessant search for significances that make it possible for this subject to live in a symbolic world is stopped, once and for all.*

I have said it thrice, therefore it is true.

March 1976
A hundred years after the publication of *The Hunting of the Snark*

NOTES

Chapter 1

1 Cause means here a condition of possibility and not a term-to-term relationship.
2 I use the concept of ego in the sense Freud gives in 'Instincts and their vicissitudes' (ibid.), without taking into account other concepts of the Ego in Freud (structural theory) or the concept of self.
3 The feeling of estrangement may be linked to the feeling of futility described by Bleger (1967), Fairbairn (1940, 1943) and Winnicott (1960a).
4 Studied by Bion (1962a, 1962b, 1965), Heimann (1943) and Klein (1946, 1952).
5 In French, 'Le temps narcissique de l'Oedipe' lends itself easily to express a 'logical' time. I prefer to leave aside the word 'time' to avoid confusion with chronological time. The word 'dimension' in English seems closer to the original sense (the narcissistic dimension of the Oedipal configuration). (See Chapters 5 and 6.)
6 From different perspectives, this has been studied by Bion (1962a) and Lacan (1966b [1956]).
7 The essays that constitute Chapters 1 and 2 are complementary, not only because they were conceived and written during the same period of time, but also because they are exploring the same clinical problems: How to listen to the patient's narcissistic mode of functioning and how to reconstruct the history of the modality thus revealed. 'The telescoping of generations' written in 1979–80 and 'Narcissistic resistances to the recognition of otherness' written in 1981 were articulated and presented in a summarized way as one lecture on November 1981 at the Paris Psychoanalytical Society under the title 'Narcissistic resistances to accepting difference between generations and otherness'. For editorial reasons, only one part was published in 1981 in French and the part concerning 'the telescoping of generations' was only published for the first time in 1985 in Spanish, after being presented in July 1985 at the International Psychoanalytical Congress in Hamburg.

Chapter 1 includes paragraphs drawn from the French and English translations that were omitted for reasons of space in the initial publication. Some errors of translation in the English version were rectified. Chapter 2 is the translation of the text published in French in 1981 with modifications coming from the aforementioned lecture. The title has been changed from the original publication.

Chapter 2

1 Psychic bisexuality is always present as an essential aspect in analysis, in particular in relation to unconscious identifications. Racism is at the narcissistic roots of rejecting differences (i.e. 'narcissism of small differences' (Freud 1918a)).

2 Given the complexity of the topic, I shall not analyse the connection between, on one hand, the pleasure–unpleasure couple and the love–hate couple and, on the other, the constitution of the ego and repression. Neither shall I discuss the parallel problem of the relationship between narcissism and the Oedipus conflict, in relation to the problem of *après-coup*. Similarly, I shall leave aside the relationship between projective identification and narcissistic resistance. Finally, the problem of unconscious identification will be dealt with only in its clinical aspect. I will simply recall the notion that identification is not considered as an initial given that does not require explanation (see Chapter 1).

3 This is a private activity of the analyst, in order to differentiate what belongs to the analyst and what belongs to the patient.

Chapter 3

1 We fear the reader may be disappointed by our way of handling the crucial problem in psychoanalysis of the relationship between material reality, psychic reality and historical reality, a relationship that exists alongside the relationship between reality and truth. A paper that concerns construction and its validation cannot circumvent this problem; however, the problem's complexity is such that it is not possible to resort to a reductionistic approach. Therefore, we shall limit ourselves to just one aspect of this complex problem, which Freud discussed throughout his work, in particular when discussing the 'primal scene' in the case of the 'Wolf Man' (1918b), and in other passages on seduction and dreams. In many cases (including our clinical material), patient and analyst share the intuition that there is a material basis for the events related; but the burden of proof (as developed here) does not consist in this intuition. Furthermore, the information produced by an outsider would not be relevant *from a psychoanalytic standpoint*, but, on the contrary, would place an obstacle in the way of discovering the *link* between material events and the patient's *psychic* structure.

Chapter 5

1 'Oedipal', when qualifying the Oedipal configuration, will be upper case.

2 A male patient, for instance, used bisexuality as a narcissistic solution to his conviction that the parents had rejected his being male. This subject is not developed here.

3 As my basic assumptions are not related to ego psychology or to self-psychology, I am not using the concept of a 'self-independent entity' or of a 'conflict-free area' of the ego; neither am I discussing the idea of an ego autonomous from the drives and from the environment. All these basic assumptions should be linked in a consistent way and it would be wrong of me to discuss any of these concepts out of context. This subject deserves a special study.

4 Since I am considering the ego as the '*total ego*' according to Freud's definition (1921: 130), I shall not specify the relations between *total ego* and *ego*, *id* and *superego*.

5 To revise from this viewpoint the ideas of different authors who have studied narcissism deserves a separate study.

6 The vignettes in Chapter 8 illustrate from a clinical standpoint the meaning I ascribe to 'intersubjectivity', in particular the idea that the intrapsychic conflict has an unconscious dimension that is revealed in the 'intersubjective' relationship. The intrapsychic dimension may be called 'intrasubjective' because there is always an 'other' who intervenes in the makeup of the patient's psyche.

7 Taking into account just for one moment Freud's structural theory, we realize that all this is linked with Freud's consideration of the child identifying with the parental *Superego*, as foreshadowed in *Group Psychology* (Freud 1921) and defined in *The Ego and the Id* (Freud 1923) as was pointed out by Roy Schafer in a personal communication after reading this essay.

8 Let us remember as well that, according to Freud, we need two essential concepts to understand the organization of the superego: (1) The concept of guilt for the murder of the father; (2) a particular psychic activity – different from repression – that leads to the resolution of the oedipal paradox and to oedipal identifications. In this perspective we can think of the relation between generations in terms of the *child's identification to the superego of the parents*. In Alice's second session we will see the protective function of superego through humour.

9 The oedipal image of the father is constructed as a consequence of this narcissistic intrapsychic struggle and the subsequent symbolic murder of the narcissistic father.

Chapter 6

1 Of course, the concept of unconscious wishes is essential. I am only trying to propose a further step.

2 When I had finished writing this essay, I became acquainted with *The Oedipus Papers* edited by George H. Pollock and John Munder Ross (1988). Luckily, I found this book when I had already finished writing my essay, because it contains so many different points that I would have thought that everything had already been said. I could not carry on the task of reading these papers and comparing our points of view. Seeing that something had been written about Laius, I read the intelligent and well-documented article written by John Munder Ross. Our theoretical perspective is different but we both give a seminal importance to filicide. Ross gives a full and, as he says, an extremely brief bibliography of those authors who have dealt with this issue. Munder Ross raises the question of whether Oedipus would have committed parricide and incest had he known the identity of his parents and

he thinks that he would not have. We have here another point of agreement. Yet there is a *theoretical* difference in our approach. Munder Ross presents this question as *contingent* in the myth. On the contrary, as we shall see, in my hypothesis parentage in itself is constitutive of the Oedipal configuration. *The unspoken message of Oedipus' history related to his genealogy, in this case his adoption, is a constitutive part of the myth.*

3 In 1967 I attended a lecture by Arnaldo and Matilde Rascovsky where filicide was pointed out in the myth. Their work has the merit of stressing filicide, but I do not feel especially close to their theoretical point of view.

4 Although a reference is made, in the interpretation of a dream referring to a (his) son's death.

5 I am leaving aside the possible interpretation according to which the two different sets of parents share a family romance, as this would require a more detailed examination and has, to my mind, no decisive implication for my hypothesis.

6 To understand the answer of the oracle, we also have to think in terms of enigma and not of riddle. Oedipus is not aware of his *unconscious question* and the answer does not speak of Oedipus' deep concern. A dialogue where the question, as well as the answer, is already an enigma is an excellent metaphor of what occurs in psychoanalysis; good interpretations do not provide *an* answer, but open new questions to be worked through.

7 This is the case of the analyst who made the comment that he could now understand why he never asked his parents any questions about what they had been doing during the war: 'I, unconsciously, already knew the answer!' Could this mean, in the myth, that Oedipus did not want to know that he had adoptive parents? Even if it could be understood as being the case, it seems to me that the following analysis stands.

8 Although I am not dealing with the problem of incest in particular (even if both desires have *necessarily* to be put together), I cannot resist the temptation of saying that once the father is *removed as a barrier* against incest (or the mother as a messenger of the threat of castration and as a messenger of the protective barrier of the superego) *incest becomes possible.*

9 The narcissistic representation in the mind – the narcissistic father – is a consequence of the narcissistic object regulation. *So we can say that a narcissistic representation in the mind needs to be metapsychologically explained* (by the functions of appropriation and intrusion).

10 Although, it must be said, in Graves' version, the second time Laius provokes Oedipus but does not try to kill him. Therefore, in this version, the logic of narcissism and of deceit is even more striking.

11 To say that I am not interested in a previous generation as *such* may seem paradoxical, insofar as I have coined the expression 'telescoping of three generations', but this concept is *not* thought of in terms of a *phylogenetic* model. As I have already worked out this problem let us just say that my main interest is the reconstruction of certain alienated identifications that encapsulate three generations as they are discovered in the history of the transference.

12 I decided not to, for the reasons I have already explained, before becoming acquainted with John Munder Ross' thoughtful work.

13 The status of the mother is not dealt with here.

14 We need a *metapsychological approach to deceit and not just a phenomenological one*. So I merely underline a theoretical problem.

15 Secrecy concerning Oedipus' adoption can be seen as destroying trust in psychic truths. Although they do not fulfil their function of deception in the same destructive way that Laius did, Polibus and Periboea failed *as messengers of a basic trust because of their own dubious status in Oedipus' filial system.*

16 In Robert Graves' English version, although the Pythoness cries the prophecy in 'disgust' ('"Away from the shrine, wretch!"', the Pythoness cried in disgust'), she uses the word 'wretch', which has two opposite meanings. According to the Collins Dictionary 'wretch' means: 1. a despicable person ('disgust'); 2. a person pitied for his misfortune (the misfortune of having a destiny that is ruled by deceit).

17 Once again, I am not taking Jocasta into account in the myth. Since in Laius' mind Jocasta has a dubious erotic status, a word should be said about the importance of the mother as the messenger who conveys to the child the existence of the father as a valid erotic husband.

Chapter 7

1 I thought out the implications of 'listening to listening' with the help of two authors. If my concept of listening to listening links up with Winnicott's concept of intersubjectivity (1967), it also takes into account Enrique Pichon-Rivière's (1957, 1960) concept of the dialectical spiral, comprising (a) the patient's words, (b) the analyst's interpretation and (c) the new emergent, that is, the patient's words after the interpretation.

2 I use *après-coup* throughout the text as it is the French equivalent of *Nachträglichkeit* and *nachträglich*. For complementary reflection of this choice and the general importance I give to this essential concept throughout the book, see Chapter 10.

3 Joyce McDougall (1989) establishes an original relationship between Ferenczi's 'wise baby' and the narcissism of the parents. She tells us that the 'wise baby' very soon learns how to cope by himself because of absent or unpredictable parents. I had up to that moment hardly concerned myself with the 'wise baby' concept. Nevertheless, I do believe that the perspective I have chosen to develop here may help to throw light on the relationship that Joyce MacDougall establishes between the 'wise baby' and parental narcissism. In other words, the 'wise baby' maintains with his parents a *paradoxical dependence* such as I have described in connection with my patient.

Chapter 8

1 How to articulate external reality, material reality and *le réel* ('the real') (Lacan)?

2 M. and W. Baranger (1961), André Green (1975), Paula Heimann (1950), Joyce McDougall (1978), Arnold Modell (1965), Michel de M'Uzan (1978), Michel Neyraut (1974), Heinrich Racker (1948, 1953, 1957), Louise de Urtubey (1994), D. W. Winnicott (1947, 1960b) and many other authors agree that the concept of countertransference is not synonymous with the analyst's neurosis. I shall not discuss this point further.

3 The 'us' points to the intersubjective transferential issue and the 'you' refers to the intrasubjective conflict.
4 I owe the concept of 'stylistic complementarity' to David Liberman (with whom I worked for many years), who must take the credit for linking psychoanalysis with linguistics and communication theory (in particular, the work of Chomsky, Jakobson and Luis Prieto).

Chapter 9

1 These ideas about the narcissistic *discourse* had been presented at the Internal Congress of the Argentine Psychoanalytical Association, November 1973 (Faimberg 1973).

Chapter 10

1 Here I write 'phantasy' to be coherent with Isaacs' way of writing according to her theoretical frame. Laplanche and Pontalis do not accept Isaacs' proposal to spell the word with 'ph' or with 'f' according to whether the fantasy is unconscious or not.
2 To avoid the term 'deferred action' other authors have recently proposed different translations: Thomä and Cheshire (*retrospective attribution* 1991), Laplanche (*afterwardsness* 1998), Modell (*retranscription of memory* 1990). See Laplanche's (1999: 263) comments on Thomä's translation.
3 In the general references I mention three essays presented on the subject (Faimberg 1998a; Green 1998 [2000]; Laplanche 1998) at the Standing Conference on Psychoanalytical Intracultural and Intercultural Dialogue held in Paris in July 1998 where the topic was 'The Concept of Temporality in French Psychoanalytical Culture'. See also Pier Luigi Rossi (1998).
4 In 2002 Laplanche gave the following definition of *après-coup*: 'The notion of *après-coup* is important for the psychoanalytical conception of temporality. It establishes a complex and reciprocal relationship between a significant event and its resignification in afterwardsness, whereby the event acquires new psychic efficiency.' *Dictionnaire international de la psychanalyse* [*International Psychoanalytical Dictionary*], Alain de Mijolla (ed.) [my translation from the French]. For the word 'afterwardsness', proposed by Laplanche, see Laplanche 1998.
5 On 6 December 1896 Freud wrote to Fliess (letter 52) as follows:

> [. . .] As you know, I am working on the assumption that our psychical mechanism has come into being by a process of stratification: the material present in the form of memory traces is being subjected from time to time to a *re-arrangement* in accordance with fresh circumstances – to a *re-transcription*. Thus what is essentially new about my theory is the thesis that memory is present not once but several times over, that it is laid down in various species of indications. I postulated a similar kind of re-arrangement some time ago (*Aphasia*) [. . .].
> (Freud 1896: 233)

Modell (1990) also studied this problem (articulated with Edelman's theories) from his own perspective.

6 Let us recall the paragraph quoted in Chapter 3.

> This second phase is the most important and the most momentous of all. But we may say of it in a certain sense that it *has never had a real existence. It is never remembered*, it has never succeeded in being conscious. It is a *construction of analysis, but it is no less a necessity* on that account.
>
> (Freud 1919a: 185 (emphasis added))

7 See, for example, ''I' Zero: Waiting' (Faimberg 1989b) (based on a short story by Italo Calvino).

8 As can be seen in the following passage, already quoted:

> By picturing our wishes as fulfilled, dreams are after all leading into the future. But this future, which the dreamer pictures as the present, has been moulded by his indestructible wish into a perfect likeness of the past.
>
> (Freud 1900: 621).

9 Nicolas Abraham and Maria Török (1978), Piera Aulagnier (1975), José Bleger (1960, 1967), André Green (1975, 1989), Jean Laplanche (1987), Jean Laplanche and Jean-Baptiste Pontalis (1964), Alain de Mijolla (1981), Enrique Pichon-Rivière (1957, 1960), and Guy Rosolato (1967), not to mention many others, are authors who have explicitly or implicitly studied this notion of the third object (from different perspectives). Michel Tort (1986) considers the third object from an epistemological standpoint.

10 On the basis of this analytical experience, as shown in this book, I proposed a definition of the 'intergenerational relationship' (1998a) included in an article I wrote for the *Dictionnaire international de la psychanalyse* on the notion of 'intergenerational' (*intergénérationnel*), where the term is always used as an adjective:

> The concept of an 'intergenerational relationship' refers to a process of (re)construction whereby a particular dimension – [which we may metaphorically call] an 'original dimension' (*l'originaire*) – is brought retroactively (*après-coup*) into existence in the history of the transference. This 'original dimension' then becomes an enabling condition for the initiation of a process of 'historicization' of the analysand in relation to two or more previous generations.

For a bibliography on the subject, see the same article.

11 It is not a phylogenetic standpoint. For the phylogenetic perspective see Faimberg (2004), Freud (1985 [1915d]) and Laplanche and Pontalis (1964).

12 Martin Wangh (1982) studies the very moment when the mechanism of disavowal is activated. Primo Levi (1986), in his extraordinary book, provides us with a profound study on the use of systematic disavowal. Robert J. Lifton (1984, 1986) helps us to understand how disavowal can be shared by so many Nazi doctors. Although Primo Levi and Lifton do not write from a psychoanalytical perspective, they offer us, as analysts, an exceptional source for reflection.

13 Freud (1911, 1915b, 1915c, 1925, 1927a); Lacan (1966b [1956]); Laplanche and Pontalis (1967).

Chapter 11

1 Curiously enough, I myself also organized this paper from the end. I first read Carroll's poem in a bad translation many years ago and the only thing I seemed to remember was the end. I read it again recently in the original version, with Gardner's valuable notes, and when arriving at the remembered end, I conceived the central thesis of the present essay.
2 'You see' (with emphasis added) indicates another two different subjects: The Author addressing the Reader.

BIBLIOGRAPHY

Abraham, N. and Török, M. (1978) *L'Écorce et le Noyau*, Paris: Aubier-Montaigne.

Anzieu, D. (1970) 'Freud et la mythologie', *Nouvelle Revue de Psychanalyse* 1: 114–45.

Aulagnier, P. (1975) *La Violence de l'Interprétation*, Paris: Presses Universitaires de France; trans. Alan Sheridan (2001) *The Violence of Interpretation*, The New Library of Psychoanalysis, London: Brunner-Routledge.

Balint, M. (1968) *The Basic Fault*, London: Tavistock.

Baranger, M. and Baranger, W. (1961) 'La situación analítica como campo dinámico', in *Problemas del Campo Analítico* (1969) Buenos Aires: Kargieman.

Baranger, W. (1961) 'El muerto vivo, estructura de los objetos en el duelo y los estados depresivos', *Revista Uruguaya de Psicoanálisis* 4: 586–603.

Bion, W. R. (1962a) *Learning from Experience*, London: Heinemann.

—— (1962b) 'A theory of thinking', *International Journal of Psychoanalysis* 43: 306–10; reprinted in *Second Thoughts* (1967) London: Heinemann.

—— (1965) *Transformations*, London: Heinemann.

—— (1967) 'Notes on memory and desire', *Psychoanalytic Forum* 2(3): 271–80.

—— (1970) 'Opacity of memory and desire', in *Attention and Interpretation*, London: Tavistock.

Bleger, J. (1960) Seminars given at the Escuela de Psiquiatría Dinámica, Buenos Aires (unpublished).

—— (1967) *Simbiosis y Ambigüedad*, Buenos Aires: Paidós.

Blum, H. (1980) 'The value of reconstruction in adult psychoanalysis', *International Journal of Psychoanalysis* 61: 39–52.

Brenman, E. (1980) 'The value of reconstruction in adult psychoanalysis', *International Journal of Psychoanalysis* 61: 53–60.

Britton, R. (1998) 'Publication anxiety', in *Belief and Imagination*, The New Library of Psychoanalysis, London and New York: Routledge.

Cahn, R. (1991) 'Du sujet', *Revue Française de Psychanalyse* 55: 1351–490.

Calvino, I. (1981) *Perché Leggere i Classici*, Milan: Palomar; reprinted (1991) Milan: Mondadori.

Carroll, L. [Dodgson, C. L.] (1876) *The Hunting of the Snark*; consulted edition, *The*

Annotated Snark (1967) Introduction and notes by M. Gardner, Harmondsworth: Penguin.

Corel, A. (1975) 'The concept of construction in Freud's work' (unpublished).

Donnet J. L. and Green, A. (1973) *L'Enfant de Ça: Pour Introduire la Psychose Blanche*, Paris: Minuit.

Faimberg, H. (1973) 'Discurso narcisista y discurso simbólico', presented at the Symposium of Argentine Psychoanalytic Association on 'La Transferencia', Buenos Aires, November 1973 (unpublished).

—— (1976) 'Richard a la luz de la guerra y de la estructura edípica', *Revista de Psicoanálisis* 33: 149–68.

—— (1989a) 'Pour une théorie (non narcissique) de l'écoute du narcissisme: Comment l'indicible devient-il dicible?', in *La Psychanalyse: Questions pour Demain* (1990) Monographies de la *Revue Française de Psychanalyse*, Paris: Presses Universitaires de France.

—— (1989b) 'T Zero: Waiting', *International Review of Psychoanalysis* 16: 101–9.

—— (1992) 'L'énigme que pose le transfert', in Jean Laplanche et al. (1994) *Colloque International de Psychanalyse*, Paris: Presses Universitaires de France.

—— (1998a) 'Après-coup', paper presented on 29 July at the IPA Standing Conference on Psychoanalytical Intracultural and Intercultural Dialogue on 'Temporality in French Psychoanalytical Culture', Paris, 27–29 July 1998.

—— (1998b) 'Reconstruction of the adolescent conflict in adult psychoanalysis', paper presented at the 'Collège Aquitain de Psychopathologie de l'Adolescent' Conference 'Être et Mal-Être à l'Adolescence', 19–20 September 1998; published in Roberto Graña and Angela Piva (eds) (2004) *Atualidade da Psicanálise de Adolescente*, São Paulo: Casa do Psicólogo.

—— (2002) 'Intergénérationnel', in A. de Mijolla (ed.) (2002) *Dictionnaire International de la Psychanalyse*, Paris: Calmann-Lévy; trans. *International Dictionary of Psychoanalysis* (2005) New York: Macmillan.

Fairbairn, W. R. D. (1940) 'Schizoid factors in the personality', in *Psychoanalytic Studies of the Personality* (1952), London: Tavistock.

—— (1943) 'The repression and the return of the bad objects', in *Psychoanalytic Studies of the Personality* (1952) London: Tavistock.

Ferenczi, S. (1923) 'The dream of the "Wise Baby"', in *Further Contributions to the Theory and Technique of Psycho-Analysis* (1980), John Rickman (ed.), Jane I. Suttie (trans.) New York: Brunner-Mazel.

Freud, S. (1895) 'Project for a scientific psychology', *The Standard Edition of the Complete Psychological Works of Sigmund Freud* (1950–74), Vol. 1, London: Hogarth Press and the Institute of Psychoanalysis.

—— (1896) Letter 52 (6 December 1896), in *Extracts from the Fliess Papers, The Standard Edition of the Complete Psychological Works of Sigmund Freud* (1950–74), Vol. 1, London: Hogarth Press and the Institute of Psychoanalysis.

—— (1897) Letter (21 September 1897), in *The Complete Letters of Sigmund Freud to Wilhem Fliess: 1887–1904* (1985), Masson J. Moussaieff (ed.) London: Harvard University Press.

—— (1899) 'Screen memories', *The Standard Edition of the Complete Psychological Works of Sigmund Freud* (1950–74), Vol. 3, London: Hogarth Press and the Institute of Psychoanalysis.

—— (1900) *The Interpretation of Dreams, The Standard Edition of the Complete Psychological*

Works of Sigmund Freud (1950–74), Vols. 4–5, London: Hogarth Press and the Institute of Psychoanalysis.

—— (1905a) *Three Essays on the Theory of Sexuality, The Standard Edition of the Complete Psychological Works of Sigmund Freud* (1950–74), Vol. 7, London: Hogarth Press and the Institute of Psychoanalysis.

—— (1905b) 'Fragments of an analysis of a case of hysteria', *The Standard Edition of the Complete Psychological Works of Sigmund Freud* (1950–74), Vol. 7, London: Hogarth Press and the Institute of Psychoanalysis.

—— (1905c) *Jokes and their Relation to the Unconscious, The Standard Edition of the Complete Psychological Works of Sigmund Freud* (1950–74), Vol. 8, London: Hogarth Press and the Institute of Psychoanalysis.

—— (1908) 'On the sexual theory of children', *The Standard Edition of the Complete Psychological Works of Sigmund Freud* (1950–74), Vol. 9, London: Hogarth Press and the Institute of Psychoanalysis.

—— (1911) 'Formulations on the two principles of mental functioning', *The Standard Edition of the Complete Psychological Works of Sigmund Freud* (1950–74), Vol. 12, London: Hogarth Press and the Institute of Psychoanalysis.

—— (1912–13) *Totem and Taboo, The Standard Edition of the Complete Psychological Works of Sigmund Freud* (1950–74), Vol. 13, London: Hogarth Press and the Institute of Psychoanalysis.

—— (1914a) 'Remembering, repeating and working-through', *The Standard Edition of the Complete Psychological Works of Sigmund Freud* (1950–74), Vol. 12, London: Hogarth Press and the Institute of Psychoanalysis.

—— (1914b) 'On narcissism: An introduction', *The Standard Edition of the Complete Psychological Works of Sigmund Freud* (1950–74), Vol. 14, London: Hogarth Press and the Institute of Psychoanalysis.

—— (1915a) 'Instincts and their vicissitudes', *The Standard Edition of the Complete Psychological Works of Sigmund Freud* (1950–74), Vol. 14, London: Hogarth Press and the Institute of Psychoanalysis.

—— (1915b) 'Repression', *The Standard Edition of the Complete Psychological Works of Sigmund Freud* (1950–74), Vol. 14, London: Hogarth Press and the Institute of Psychoanalysis.

—— (1915c) 'The unconscious', *The Standard Edition of the Complete Psychological Works of Sigmund Freud* (1950–74), Vol. 14, London: Hogarth Press and the Institute of Psychoanalysis.

—— (1917a) 'Mourning and melancholia', *The Standard Edition of the Complete Psychological Works of Sigmund Freud* (1950–74), Vol. 14, London: Hogarth Press and the Institute of Psychoanalysis.

—— (1917b) 'A difficulty in the path of psychoanalysis', *The Standard Edition of the Complete Psychological Works of Sigmund Freud* (1950–74), Vol. 17, London: Hogarth Press and the Institute of Psychoanalysis.

—— (1918a) 'The taboo of virginity', *The Standard Edition of the Complete Psychological Works of Sigmund Freud* (1950–74), Vol. 11, London: Hogarth Press and the Institute of Psychoanalysis.

—— (1918b) *From the History of an Infantile Neurosis* (The Wolf Man), *The Standard Edition of the Complete Psychological Works of Sigmund Freud* (1950–74), Vol. 17, London: Hogarth Press and the Institute of Psychoanalysis.

—— (1919a) 'A child is being beaten', *The Standard Edition of the Complete Psychological Works of Sigmund Freud* (1950–74), Vol. 17, London: Hogarth Press and the Institute of Psychoanalysis.

—— (1919b) 'The uncanny', *The Standard Edition of the Complete Psychological Works of Sigmund Freud* (1950–74), Vol. 17, London: Hogarth Press and the Institute of Psychoanalysis.

—— (1920) *Beyond the Pleasure Principle, The Standard Edition of the Complete Psychological Works of Sigmund Freud* (1950–74), Vol. 18, London: Hogarth Press and the Institute of Psychoanalysis.

—— (1921) *Group Psychology and the Analysis of the Ego, The Standard Edition of the Complete Psychological Works of Sigmund Freud* (1950–74), Vol. 18, London: Hogarth Press and the Institute of Psychoanalysis.

—— (1923) 'The ego and the id', *The Standard Edition of the Complete Psychological Works of Sigmund Freud* (1950–74), Vol. 19, London: Hogarth Press and the Institute of Psychoanalysis.

—— (1924) 'The economic problem of masochism', *The Standard Edition of the Complete Psychological Works of Sigmund Freud* (1950–74), Vol. 19, London: Hogarth Press and the Institute of Psychoanalysis.

—— (1925) 'Negation', *The Standard Edition of the Complete Psychological Works of Sigmund Freud* (1950–74), Vol. 19, London: Hogarth Press and the Institute of Psychoanalysis.

—— (1927a) 'Fetishism', *The Standard Edition of the Complete Psychological Works of Sigmund Freud* (1950–74), Vol. 21, London: Hogarth Press and the Institute of Psychoanalysis.

—— (1927b) 'Humour', *The Standard Edition of the Complete Psychological Works of Sigmund Freud* (1950–74), Vol. 21, London: Hogarth Press and the Institute of Psychoanalysis.

—— (1937) 'Constructions in analysis', *The Standard Edition of the Complete Psychological Works of Sigmund Freud* (1950–74), Vol. 23, London: Hogarth Press and the Institute of Psychoanalysis.

—— (1940 [1938a]) 'An outline of psychoanalysis', *The Standard Edition of the Complete Psychological Works of Sigmund Freud* (1950–74), Vol. 23, London: Hogarth Press and the Institute of Psychoanalysis.

—— (1940 [1938b]) 'Splitting of the ego in the process of defence', *The Standard Edition of the Complete Psychological Works of Sigmund Freud* (1950–74), Vol. 23, London: Hogarth Press and the Institute of Psychoanalysis.

—— (1985 [1915d]) *A Phylogenetic Fantasy: Overview of the Transference Neurosis*, Ilse Grubrich-Simitis (ed.), Cambridge, MA: Belknap Press of Harvard University Press.

Gardner, M. (ed.) (1967) *The Annotated Snark*, London: Penguin.

Graves, R. (1955) *The Greek Myths*, Vol. 2, London: Penguin.

Green, A. (1966) 'L'objet (a) de J. Lacan, sa logique et la théorie freudienne', *Cahiers de l'Analyse* 3: 15–37.

—— (1973) *Le Discours Vivant*, Paris: Presses Universitaires de France.

—— (1975) 'The analyst, symbolization, and absence in the analytic setting', *International Journal of Psychoanalysis* 56: 1–22; reprinted in *Private Madness* (1986) London: Hogarth Press.

—— (1989) 'Du tiers', in *La Psychanalyse: Questions pour Demain*, Monographies de la *Revue Française de Psychanalyse*, Paris: Presses Universitaires de France.

—— (1998) 'Le temps éclaté', paper presented at the IPA Standing Conference on Psychoanalytical Intracultural and Intercultural Dialogue, Paris, 27–29 July 1998.

—— (2000) *Le Temps Éclaté*, Paris: Minuit; trans. *Time in Psychoanalysis* (2002) London: Free Association Books.

Heimann, P. (1943) 'Certain functions of introjection and projection in early infancy', in M. Klein, P. Heimann, S. Isaacs and J. Rivière (eds) (1952) *Developments in Psychoanalysis*, London: Hogarth Press.

—— (1950) 'On counter-transference', *International Journal of Psychoanalysis* 31: 81–4.

Isaacs, S. (1948) 'The nature and function of phantasy', *International Journal of Psychoanalysis*, 29: 73–97, reprinted in M. Klein, P. Heimann, S. Isaacs and J. Rivière (eds) (1952) *Developments in Psychoanalysis*. London: Hogarth Press.

Klein, M. (1945) 'The Oedipus complex in the light of early anxieties', in *Contributions to Psychoanalysis*, London: Hogarth Press.

—— (1946) 'Notes on some schizoid mechanisms', in M. Klein, P. Heimann, S. Isaacs and J. Rivière (eds) (1952) *Developments in Psychoanalysis*, London: Hogarth Press.

—— (1952) 'Some theoretical conclusions regarding the emotional life of the infant', in M. Klein, P. Heimann, S. Isaacs and J. Rivière (eds) (1952) *Developments in Psychoanalysis*, London: Hogarth Press.

Lacan, J. (1965) 'La science et la vérité', in *Écrits* (1966) Paris: Seuil.

—— (1966a [1953]) 'The function and field of speech and language in psychoanalysis', in *Écrits: A Selection*, trans. Alan Sheridan, London: Tavistock.

—— (1966b [1956]) 'Réponse au commentaire de Jean Hyppolite sur la *Verneinung*', in *Écrits* (1966) Paris: Seuil.

—— (1996 [1955–6]), 'On a question preliminary to any possible treatment of psychosis', in *Écrits: A Selection*, trans. Alan Sheridan, London: Tavistock.

—— (1966) *Écrits*, Paris: Seuil.

—— (1977) *Écrits: A Selection*, trans. Alan Sheridan, London: Tavistock.

Laplanche, J. (1987) *New Foundations for Psychoanalysis* (1989) trans. D. Macey, Oxford: Blackwell.

—— (1998) 'Notes sur l'après-coup', paper presented at the IPA Standing Conference on Psychoanalytical Intracultural and Intercultural dialogue, Paris, 27–29 July 1998; published in John Fletcher and Martin Stanton (eds) (1992) *Seduction, Translation and the Drives*, London: Institute of Contemporary Arts; also in *Essays on Otherness* (1999), London: Routledge.

—— (2002) 'Après-coup', in A. de Mijolla (ed.) *Dictionnaire International de la Psychanalyse*, Paris: Calmann-Lévy; trans. *International Dictionary of Psychoanalysis* (2005) New York: Macmillan.

Laplanche, J. and Pontalis, J.-B. (1964) 'Fantasme originaire, fantasmes des origines, origine du fantasme', in *Les Temps Modernes* 19 (215); trans. 'Fantasy and the origins of sexuality', *International Journal of Psychoanalysis* 49: 1–18.

—— (1967) *Vocabulaire de la Psychanalyse*, Paris: Presses Universitaires de France; trans. D. Nicholson Smith (1983) *The Language of Psycho-Analysis*, London: Hogarth Press.

Leclaire, S. (1971) *Démasquer le Réel*, Paris: Seuil.

Levi, P. (1986) *The Drowned and the Saved*, trans. (1988) London: Michael Joseph.

Liberman, D. (1970) *Lingüística, Interacción Comunicativa, Proceso Psicoanalítico,* Buenos Aires: Galerna.

Lifton, R. J. (1984) 'Medicalized killing in Auschwitz', in *Psychoanalytic Reflections on the Holocaust,* Selected Essays, Steven Leuel and Paul Marcus (eds) (1984) New York: Ktav and University of Denver.

—— (1986) *The Nazi Doctors,* New York: Basic.

Loewald, H. W. (1951) 'Ego and reality', in *Papers on Psychoanalysis* (1980) New Haven and London: Yale University Press.

McDougall, J. (1978) 'Le contretransfert et la commnication primitive', in *Plaidoyer pour une Certaine Anormalité,* 117–38, Paris: Gallimard; trans. *Plea for a Measure of Abnormality* (1980) New York: International Universities Press; reprinted (1990) London: Free Association Books.

—— (1989) 'Le rêve et le psychosoma', in *La Psychanalyse: Questions Pour Demain,* Monographies de la *Revue Française de Psychoanalyse,* Paris: Presses Universitaires de France.

Maci, G. (1979) 'Dialéctica de los espacios interior y exterior', in *La Otra Escena de lo Real,* Buenos Aires: Nueva Visión.

Mijolla, A. de (1981) *Les Visiteurs de Moi,* Paris: Les Belles Lettres.

—— (ed.) (2002) *Dictionnaire International de la Psychanalyse,* Paris: Calmann-Lévy; trans. *International Dictionary of Psychoanalysis* (2005) New York: Macmillan.

Milner, M. (1934) *A Life of One's Own,* London: Chatto & Windus.

—— (1952) 'Aspects of symbolism in comprehension of the not-self', *International Journal of Psychoanalysis* 33: 181; reprinted in M. Klein, P. Heimann and R. Money-Kyrle (eds) (1955) *New Directions in Psycho-Analysis* London: Tavistock.

Modell, A. H. (1965) 'On having the right to a living: An aspect of the super-ego development', *International Journal of Psychoanalysis* 46: 323–31.

—— (1984) *Psychoanalysis in a New Context,* New York: International Universities Press.

—— (1990) *Other Times, Other Realities,* Cambridge, MA: Harvard University Press.

Mom, J. (1960) 'Aspectos teóricos y técnicos de las fobias y en las modalidades fóbicas', *Revista de Psicoanálisis* 17: 190–215.

M'Uzan, M. de (1978) 'La bouche de l'inconscient', *Nouvelle Revue de Psychanalyse* 17: 87–9.

Neyraut, M. (1974) *Le Transfert,* Paris: Presses Universitaires de France.

—— (1978) *Les Logiques de l'Inconscient,* Paris: Hachette.

—— (1997) 'Considérations rétrospectives sur "l'après-coup"', *Revue Française de Psychanalyse* 61: 1247–54.

Pichon-Rivière, E. (1957) Seminars given at the Asociacion Psicoanalítica Argentina, in *Teoría del Vínculo* (1980) Buenos Aires: Nueva Vísion.

—— (1960) Seminars given at the Escuela de Psiquiatría Dinámica, Buenos Aires (unpublished).

Pollock, G. H. and Munder Ross, J. (eds) (1988) *The Oedipus Papers,* Madison, CT: International Universities Press.

Racker, H. (1948) 'Neurosis of countertransference', in *Transference and Countertransference* (1968) New York: International Universities Press.

—— (1953) 'The meanings and uses of countertransference', in *Transference and Countertransference* (1968) New York: International Universities Press.

—— (1957) *Estudios Sobre Técnica Psicoanalítica*, Buenos Aires: Paidós; trans. *Transference and Countertransference* (1968) New York: International Universities Press.

Reik, T. (1935) *Surprise and the Psycho-Analyst*, London: Kegan Paul.

Rivière, J. (1936) 'A contribution to the analysis of the negative therapeutic reaction', *International Journal of Psychoanalysis* 17: 304–20.

Rosolato, G. (1967) 'Trois générations d'hommes dans le mythe religieux et dans la généalogie', *L'Inconscient* 1: 71–108.

Rossi, P. L. (1998) 'Gli approcci teorico-clinici francesi alla temporalità e la sua costruzione nel processo psicoanalitico', *Rivista di Psicoanalisi* 44: 631–5.

Sandler, J. and Sandler, A.-M. (1987) 'The past unconscious, the present unconscious and the vicissitudes of guilt', *International Journal of Psychoanalysis* 68: 331–41.

—— (1994) 'The past unconscious and the present unconscious', *Psychoanalytic Study of the Child* 49: 278–92.

Strachey, J. (1934) 'The nature of the therapeutic action of psycho-analysis', *International Journal of Psychoanalysis* 15: 127–59.

Thomä, H. and Cheshire, N. (1991) 'Freud's concept of *Nachträglichkeit* and Strachey's "deferred action": Trauma, constructions and the direction of causality', *International Review of Psychoanalysis* 3: 401–45.

Tort, M. (1986) 'L'argument généalogique', *Topique* 38.

Urtubey, L. de (1994) 'Le travail du contretransfert', *Revue Française de Psychanalyse* 58: 1271–372.

Viderman, S. (1970) *La Construction de l'Espace Analytique*, Paris: Denoël.

Wangh, M. (1982) 'On obstacles to the working-through of the Nazi Holocaust experience and on the consequences of failing to do so', in S. A. Luel and P. Marcus (eds) (1984) *Psychoanalytical Reflexions on the Holocaust*, New York: Ktav and University of Denver.

Winnicott, D. W. (1947) 'Hate in the countertransference', in *D. W. Winnicott: Collected Papers* (1958) London: Tavistock.

—— (1953) 'Transitional objects and transitional phenomena', in *Playing and Reality* (1971) London: Tavistock.

—— (1960a) 'True and false self', in *The Maturational Processes and the Facilitating Environment* (1979) London: Hogarth Press.

—— (1960b) 'Countertransference', in *The Maturational Processes and the Facilitating Environment* (1979) London: Hogarth Press.

—— (1967) 'Mirror role of mother and family in child development', in *Playing and Reality* (1971) London: Tavistock.

—— (1974) 'Fear of breakdown', *International Review of Psychoanalysis* 1: 103–7.

INDEX

absence, psychic 4, 6–8, 12, 18, 46–7;
  and overpresent object 8; *see also*
  unconscious identification/s
absent concept 43, 114
absent object as a psychoanalytical object
  87
adolescence and (re)construction in adult
  analysis 109; Brigitte 95–6; Maryse 93
affirmation, basic 18 (*Bejahung*)
agony, primitive (Winnicott) and
  après-coup 110; *see also* anxiety, dread
Alice: changes of relationship with
  objects 60–2; disavowal of
  helplessness 53–5; grandparent as
  narcissistic parent 60, 61; infantile
  sexual theory 55, and phallic logic
  (intelligence/stupidity, not asking
  questions) 53, 54, 55, 61; internal
  mother 54, 55; interpretative style
  53–5; intrapsychic unconscious reality
  61, 62, 114; narcissistic dimension of
  oedipal rivalry (mother/sister) 55, 57;
  parents' sexuality 60–2; private
  language 53, 54, 55; silence/
  inaccessibility and narcissistic
  paradoxical transference 52, 55, 58;
  telescoping of three generations 54,
  55–6, 60, 61; third object of the other
  114; third position 52, 53, 54;
  unconscious scene 54, 55; *see also*
  narcissistic dimension of Oedipal
  configuration

alienated adaptation 9, 10, 11, 12
alienated/alienation, ego 8–11, 13, 15,
  17–18, 112–13, 115; *see also*
  disidentification; splitting
alienated unconscious narcissistic
  identifications 115; *see also*
  identification/s
alliance, fraternal 38, 59; *see also*
  intersubjectivity; object relations;
  otherness; *Totem and Taboo*
analysand: discourse 45, 95;
  dissymmetrical position 43, 91;
  narcissistic regulation 30, 58, 60;
  narcissistic resistances 22–3, 25, 30;
  reciprocal fascination illusion 22–3,
  79, 81; silence 22, 23, 47, 81;
  transformation/change 60–1, 81, 89;
  unconscious guilt 49; vignettes *see*
  case studies; *see also* history
analyst: analysis of 45, 91;
  beliefs/illusions modification 8, 22;
  clinical experience 2; complementary
  identification 12, 48; desire 15;
  dissymmetrical position 43, 91;
  narcissistic field 81; narcissistic
  resistances 22–3, 30, 44, 101–7;
  Oedipal structure (Racker) 42;
  personal characteristics 45; position
  43, 91; reciprocal fascination illusion
  22–3, 79, 81; self-analysis/reflection
  46, 47; silence 2, 23, 24, 25;
  theoretical position 45, 48, 79, 81,